The CRYSTAL COLLECTOR

The CRYSTAL COLLECTOR

HOW TO BUILD A LIFELONG COLLECTION OF CRYSTALS AND STONES

Jillian Aurelia Green

DAVID & CHARLES

www.davidandcharles.com

David and Charles is an imprint of David and Charles, Ltd
Suite A, Tourism House, Pynes Hill, Exeter, EX2 5WS

Conceived, edited, and designed by Quarto Publishing, an imprint of
The Quarto Group, 1 Triptych Place, London, SE1 9SH

First published in the UK and USA in 2024

A catalogue record for this book is available from the British Library.

ISBN-13: 9781446313374 paperback
ISBN-13: 9781446313381 EPUB

This book has been printed on paper from approved suppliers and made from
pulp from sustainable sources.

Printed in China.

10 9 8 7 6 5 4 3 2 1

Editor: Charlene Fernandes
Copyeditor: Caroline West
Editorial assistant: Elinor Ward
Art director: Martina Calvio
Research assistant: Oliver Luke Delorie
Designer (layout): Eleanor Ridsdale Colussi
Designer: Eliana Holder
Photography: Dave Burton and Jess Esposito (crystals),
Hannah Cohen (author photo), other photography (see page 144)
Publisher: Lorraine Dickey

David and Charles publishes high-quality books on a wide range of subjects.
For more information visit www.davidandcharles.com.

Follow us on Instagram by searching for @dandcbooks_wellbeing.

Layout of the digital edition of this book may vary depending on reader
hardware and display settings.

CONTENTS

MEET JILLIAN

I began writing this book during a time of great upheaval in my life, all while managing my company alone for the first time in half a decade. Yet, as they always have been, the stones were there for me.

Writing in stolen moments between meetings and in early mornings before work began, the crystals were there to comfort me, embolden me, and bring me back to myself.

And for that I am so grateful.

Like many others, I found that crystals always called to me. I was fascinated by caves and mines as a child; I collected stones wherever I went and had my favorites on a makeshift altar in my closet. I loved the way they could make me feel—safe, calm, confident, or joyous. I found a little leather pouch in a store and created a talisman bag, so I could always keep my crystals near me when I ventured out into the sometimes overwhelming world. I felt as if the stones were always whispering their stories and secrets to me, and if I was quiet enough, I could hear them.

I'm grateful now for the opportunity to share some of their wisdom, as well as the knowledge I have acquired over my lifetime of how to consciously source, connect with, and care for these beautiful crystal beings. Whether you are just beginning your crystalline journey, have a few stones but want to understand them better, or you have a large collection but are unsure how to safeguard and preserve it, my hope is this book will be helpful to you.

Jillian Aurelia Green

1 BUILDING YOUR CRYSTAL COLLECTION

The crystals we decide to add to our collection is a deeply personal choice. We may purchase a specific specimen due to its unique qualities, or because of its metaphysical properties, or simply because we find it beautiful. Whatever the reason we're drawn to a piece, it's only too easy to forget that crystals have been on their own journey long before they came into our lives.

Understanding how these special stones made their way from the depths of the Earth into our hands is just as important as knowing how to work with and care for them once we've brought them home. To that end, this book begins by exploring where crystals come from, how they are mined and carved, and how to differentiate between authentic stones and those that have been treated or manufactured.

When we have greater awareness of the crystals within our collection, as well as the wider crystal industry as a whole, we are empowered to make choices that resonate with our values, beneficially support those miners and carvers who once held the crystals we love, and ultimately raise the vibration of our own lives.

HOW TO KNOW WHEN A CRYSTAL IS MEANT FOR YOU

Knowing when a crystal is meant for your collection is a choice you must make yourself. While some base their decision on value, beauty, or rarity, many choose their crystal companions according to which they feel most drawn toward, or most align with what they wish to attract, heal, or manifest.

RARITY

Some collectors choose crystals, minerals, or specimens specifically because of the rarity of the piece. Rare stones derive their worth from scarcity, or striking attributes like color, size, clarity, or the way they have been cut or carved. Uncommon inclusions, variations, or localities can contribute to the desirability of a stone, while historical or cultural significance can amplify the attraction of having the stone in your collection. Untreated crystals and gemstones are particularly valued, and collectors are drawn to them for their investment potential, the captivating beauty they offer, the rich narratives they carry, their exclusivity, and the personal passion they ignite. As both investments and treasures, these stones occupy a special place in the realm of gem collecting, captivating enthusiasts with their rarity and intrinsic allure.

AESTHETIC

How a piece looks often plays a significant role in crystal selection. Some will choose a stone for its clarity, shimmer, flash, or brilliant inner rainbows. Others gravitate toward stones in their favorite color, or with regards to gemstone jewelry, whether the tones or aesthetic of a crystal match their day-to-day style. Still others choose crystals based on their visual appeal, either finding them beautiful or appreciating how certain stones complement their home decor, or arouse a sense of harmony and beauty in their living or work environment. Whether worn, displayed, or just enjoyed, the visual appearance of the stone is the overriding factor in why it was acquired.

METAPHYSICAL BENEFIT

As spirituality and magic have become mainstream, the focus of collecting minerals for solely aesthetic or investment purposes has shifted to the metaphysical benefit stones can provide. While the colors and individual features may draw someone to select a specific piece, the reason a crystal is sought out in the first place is because its energetic properties align with what they wish to call into their life. Just remember that although books or teachers may recommend distinct stones for certain ailments, growth opportunities, or situations, always trust your intuition first and foremost. You know yourself better than anyone else. If you feel a crystal will benefit you, then listen carefully to your inner wisdom.

EMOTIONAL/ENERGETIC CONNECTION

Most often, people choose to adopt a particular stone because it makes them feel a certain way, or those who are energy-sensitive might feel called to or connected with an individual cluster, tower, tumble, or sphere. Crystals resonate on an energetic and emotional level, and when held or placed nearby can offer comfort, calmness, or a sense of empowerment. This personal connection creates a profound bond, making the stone a beautiful source of solace, support, and positive energy.

WHAT'S IN A STONE'S NAME?

Trade Names, Trademarked Names, and Mineralogical Names

The taxonomy and nomenclature of the crystal world can be incredibly confusing. Some crystal names stretch back thousands of years to ancient Rome, Egypt, Greece, and India (e.g. amethyst); some are simply named after the locality in which they were initially found (e.g. labradorite), their appearance (e.g. astrophyllite), and commonly, the first non-Indigenous explorer, miner, or scientist to "discover" them (e.g. bornite). Even ignoring linguistic translations, many stones have developed multiple names based on how they look, their metaphysical properties, mistaken identities, or even marketing purposes.

Here is a case in point: the steppes of Argentina produce a beautiful, teal-blue calcite that actually has two trade names: *Blue Onyx* and *Blue Aragonite*. Neither of these are accurate as the crystal is neither onyx, nor aragonite. Meanwhile, it was recently trademarked as Lemurian Aquatine Calcite™. Which of these names is correct? Technically, none of them, yet all are commonly used to refer to this Patagonian blue calcite.

TRADE NAMES

Trade names are monikers given to crystals by individuals, businesses, or communities to express their physical attributes or metaphysical benefits, or to enhance their desirability. These names are not officially recognized by mineralogists, but are used to differentiate between new combinations of minerals or those from specific localities, and to make specific crystals more appealing or distinctive.

Here are a few examples:
Quantum Quattro—Copper-mineral combination of chrysocolla, dioptase, malachite, shattuckite, and quartz from Namibia.
Fire and Ice Quartz—Low-grade quartz that is heated and rapidly cooled in a lab to produce a crackle effect (that is, crackle quartz).
Bolivianite—May refer to ametrine (amethyst/citrine), or the combination of green serpentine and purple fluorite, although both stones can be found outside of Bolivia.

TRADEMARKED NAMES

Trademarked names are legally protected names or symbols that are used to represent a specific brand or company. In the context of the crystal industry, some companies, mines, or miners may trademark specific names to distinguish their crystals in the market. This adds an extra layer of exclusivity and recognition, but can also create tension in crystal communities if someone trademarks a new name for a stone that already exists in order to capitalize on its metaphysical benefits, charge a higher price, or in an attempt to corner the market by barring others from utilizing the trademarked name.

Ocean Jasper™—An orbicular jasper from Madagascar, also known as sea jasper.
Atlantasite™—A stone combination consisting of serpentine and stichtite.
Mystic Merlinite™—A black and lilac-gray stone comprising feldspars, quartz, and micas; more commonly referred to as indigo gabbro.

MINERALOGICAL NAMES

Mineralogical names are scientifically recognized labels for crystals, minerals, and stones. As of 1960, every new find must be submitted to the International Mineralogical Association (IMA) and approved by the Commission on New Minerals and Mineral Names (CNMNC), which is also the deciding factor on official names for previously discovered stones that may have multiple aliases. Often ending in "-ite," from the Greek adjective for "stone," the name is typically derived from its appearance, locality, composition, or the last name of its "discoverer." (e.g. azurite, from the Arabic word for blue).

The mineralogical name becomes standardized and universally accepted in the field of mineralogy, with only minor variations attributed to differing languages. This "official" name is used to describe the mineral species without any marketing or branding influence.

Quartz—One of the most common minerals on Earth, with the name derived from a German word for "hard."
Shattuckite—A blue copper silicate hydroxide originally found at the Shattuck Mine, in Arizona.
Titanite—Previously known (and still commonly referred to) as sphene, the Commission opted for titanite, which is now the official name of this calcium titanium stone.

▶ This beautiful blue stone has had a few different names since its discovery in 1791. Originally dubbed *fasriger schwerspath*, it was renamed *schwefelsaurer strontianite aus Pennsylvania*, and then again in 1798 to the German *zoelestin*, or celestine, in English. Celestine was later changed to celestite to match the common -ite form of mineral names. However, the IMA changed it back to the original English name, celestine, in the mid-1980s. Both names are still commonly used.

HOW TO KNOW WHAT YOU'RE BUYING: TREATED & SIMULATED CRYSTALS

While some treated crystals are highly sought after, most are used to dupe buyers. If a crystal looks too perfect, or is priced too low, it may be treated, or simply made of glass or plastic. When in doubt, look for the features, "flaws," striations, and growth patterns that make each piece unique.

COMMONLY TREATED CRYSTALS

Natural Smoky Quartz versus Irradiated Smoky Quartz

Natural smoky quartz forms when clear quartz is exposed to natural radiation over millions of years. Ranging in shade from very pale to root-beer dark, smoky quartz often exhibits variations in transparency and phantoms. Irradiated smoky quartz, on the other hand, is blasted with radiation in a lab to enhance its color, resulting in a uniform, very dark hue. It is safe to assume that most lighter and medium shades of smoky quartz are natural. In darker saturations, look for variabilities in color zoning and/or phantoms to authenticate.

Natural Citrine versus Baked Amethyst versus Lemon Quartz

Natural citrine ranges in hue from pale honey to deep golden, and gains its color organically due to the presence of heat and pressure. Natural citrine typically grows as points, or in specialized formations such as Abundance, Candle, Castle, Cathedral, or Elestial. Baked amethyst, often sold as citrine, is heat-treated, and displays an orange to brownish color, and is usually found in small-pointed clusters or tooth-like points. Lemon quartz, an irradiated variety of quartz, is a transparent lemony-yellow silicate that is rarely found in nature and is almost exclusively lab-treated. The color and formation are the easiest ways to differentiate true citrine from the two imposters.

Natural Aura (Limonite) versus Treated Aura

Natural aura, also known as limonite aura, exhibits a range of earthy, metallic colors like gold, green, or red. These hues result from natural, metal-rich mineral deposits on the crystal's surface. Treated aura, conversely, undergoes a process where metals are bonded to the crystal's surface in a lab, creating an iridescent rainbow sheen that appears artificially vibrant and uniform. Natural limonite aura lacks the uniformity of the treated version, so if it looks overly vibrant and consistent, it has most likely been treated.

Natural Turquoise versus Stabilized versus Reconstituted versus Dyed Howlite

Natural turquoise displays an organic texture with visible matrix lines. Stabilized turquoise is common within the jewelry world and impregnated with resin for enhanced hardness while maintaining its natural features and coloring. Reconstituted turquoise is composed of pulverized natural turquoise mixed with binding agents for a uniform look. Dyed howlite mimics turquoise's natural veining, but is a white stone that has been dyed blue to imitate it. If the price seems very low, it is most likely howlite or reconstituted turquoise. Be sure to examine texture, color, and consistency, and ask about the locality and treatment before adding a piece to your collection.

Further Fakes to Watch Out For

Treated:

Agates Often dyed in bright colors such as blue, teal, purple, or pink.

Amber Amber with glittery "sun spots" has been heat-treated, or reconstituted.

Blue topaz Heated to turn blue or pink. Avoid vibrant colors.

Howlite Dyed to fake other colored crystals.

Jadeite Sometimes bleached and impregnated with resin to appear higher grade. Certified A-grade jadeite is untreated.

Lapis lazuli Some low-grade lapis lazuli is dyed a darker blue.

Prasiolite Heat treatment can create this "green amethyst."

Tanzanite Often heat-treated to create a more vibrant shade of blue.

Manufactured and faked:

Bismuth Lab-grown rainbow metallic crystal

Cherry quartz Man-made, red, swirled glass

Gold stone Shimmering, red or blue glass with flecks of sparkles similar to aventurines

Green phantom "ghost" quartz clusters Lab-grown, these have dark green tips and appear "frosted" with smaller crystals.

Hematite Magnetic hematite isn't actually hematite, but manufactured.

Moldavite An expensive and rare tektite now commonly copied using green glass

Opalite Pearlescent, man-made glass

METHODS OF TESTING FOR AUTHENTICITY

Visual/Tactile Test

The safest test on the list is simply to use your eyes. Research the important signifiers of the stone you want to authenticate and check to see if your piece has them. For example, falsified moldavite is made of a green glass that is shinier and more uniform, and lacks the trademark bubbles and imperfections typically found within true moldavite.

Scratch Test

Utilize the Mohs scale to assess the hardness of the crystal. Crystals with a Mohs hardness of 1–2 are soft enough to be scratched by a fingernail. Crystals with 3–5 hardness are medium and can be scratched by metal. Crystals with a 6–9 rating typically cannot be scratched by metal, but can scratch glass, while diamond, a 10 on the Mohs scale, is the hardest known mineral and can only be scratched by itself. A scratch test can also determine if a crystal has been coated with epoxy, dye, or metal oxide (aura quartz).

Ultraviolet Light Test

Many natural crystals such as ruby or mangano calcite exhibit fluorescence under ultraviolet light. UV reactions in imposter stones can be difficult to falsify.

Specific Gravity Test

Compare the weight of the crystal to its volume by submerging it in water. Different minerals have different specific gravities. Remember to only use this method on water-safe stones!

Heat Test

Extreme heat can damage or fade fake or dyed crystals, while natural ones are generally more heat-resistant. Please research how to test your crystals safely before pursuing.

Refractive Index

Different minerals have distinct refractive indices. Using a refractometer, you can measure the refractive index of your crystal to authenticate it.

Consult an Expert

Seek advice from a certified gemologist or a reputable crystal expert, especially for high-value or rare specimens, and be careful when testing or attempting to authenticate crystals, especially if they are valuable or delicate. When in doubt, always consult an expert.

◀ Brilliantly colored crystals can occur naturally, but more often than not they signify stones that have been dyed or treated.

HOW TO SOURCE CRYSTALS FOR YOUR COLLECTION

I remember as a kid I loved visiting museums, in part because I loved learning, but I also knew the gift store would inevitably have crystals, rocks, and geodes. I'd spend ages picking through tubs of multi-stone mixes to find just the right tumble to take home with me.

While jewelry was easier to find, unless you were part of a rockhounding club or directly involved in the industry, the opportunity to acquire crystals used to be rather limited to museums, metaphysical stores, or specialized mineral boutiques, or would involve traveling to gem shows or heading into nature in the hopes of finding them yourself.

As technology has evolved and the popularity of crystal collecting has grown, however, so too has accessibility. While finding additions to your collection in person is still a rewarding experience, nowadays it's just as easy, if not easier, to find your new favorite stone online or through social media. Whether you're just starting out or are a seasoned collector, these are the five most common ways to source your new stones:

GEM SHOWS

Gem shows are my absolute favorite way to source crystals for both my store and my personal collection. Ranging from small, local community events to huge multi-week showcases such as in Tucson or Munich, gem shows are incredible for their ability to bring together miners, makers, and vendors from all over the world. While some shows are reserved for wholesalers, many are open to the public, and present an opportunity for you to be viscerally immersed in the sheer variety of crystals, minerals, and specimens this amazing planet has to offer.

With so much available, gem shows are a wonderful way to discover new crystals you've never even heard of, or find that elusive missing piece from your collection (I'm looking at you ajoite), all at a typically lower price point than in a store since you're purchasing directly from the miners, carvers, or importers.

I also think gem shows are one of the best ways to learn more about the crystals you may be interested in or already have: not only do vendors have some spectacular stories to tell, but having so much choice and variety means you're able to compare different levels of grade and quality, understand why a specific locality of a specimen is more expensive than another, and experience the magic of specialty pieces unavailable anywhere else. Plus, those crystal bathtubs and two-story-tall geodes found at larger showcases make for some amazing photo and selfie opportunities.

If you love crystals, visiting a gem show at least once is a must.

CRYSTAL STORES

Many people, especially those selecting stones for their metaphysical benefits, prefer to choose their crystals in person. Photos can be edited, but when you lay eyes on a specimen in a glass case or hold a palm stone in your hand, you're able to experience the crystal for yourself. While shopping in person might be a little more expensive due to overhead costs like rent and staff, supporting your local crystal store gives you the opportunity to find your perfect tumble, try on bracelets or other jewelry, feel a stone's effect on you in real time, and make connections with others who love crystals as much as you— all without having to travel far to do so.

Once a staple of New Age and metaphysical communities, crystal stores have become more prevalent, with many traditional home decor outlets, book stores, and even clothing stores now carrying an assortment of popular stones. If you're the naturally curious type, or if conscious sourcing is something that is important to you, I'd recommend sticking to specialized boutiques, as they should be able to more thoroughly answer questions about geology and sourcing, as well as provide recommendations.

ECOMMERCE

If you don't have a local crystal, mineral, or metaphysical store nearby, the internet can be a fantastic resource for purchasing new stones. With thousands of websites to explore, many with specialties, you certainly aren't lacking in choice for options, and many sites today even feature metaphysical as well as geological information to help you make your decisions.

There is, however, one huge caveat: crystal selling has grown exponentially in the last few years on popular sites like Etsy and eBay, but with their rise so too has the spread of misinformation and, frankly, blatant lies. These sites make it easy to find specific crystals through powerful and easy-to-navigate search engines, but they also enable anyone to begin selling without any prior knowledge. Many of the sellers don't actually know anything about stones or care how they're procured. I can't tell you how often I'll notice blue calcite being referred to as celestite, or chrysocolla in quartz as quantum quattro. eBay is filled with fake and treated crystals being advertised as natural and real. Not all ecommerce sellers are mislabeling purposely, but doing your own due diligence is paramount.

If you're unsure about a crystal seller's knowledge or legitimacy, it's often safer to stick to those e-shops with high ratings, or established crystal and mineral companies that have their own websites, as they are typically fully invested in the industry.

SOCIAL MEDIA

In only a few short years, shopping via social media has become one of the most popular and accessible ways to purchase crystals for a collection. From your own phone you're able to connect to thousands of crystal stores around the world and easily see what they have on offer. While brick-and-mortar stores might sometimes be limited in their offerings, a simple hashtag search can help you find a vendor offering the exact rare specimen you've been after. Streaming live sales are the next best thing to buying crystals in person, as you're able to see the specific stones you're interested in purchasing and ask the curator questions about particular pieces in real time, all while sitting on your own couch.

The downside is that the algorithm often determines which stones or crystal vendors you're able to see in your feed, which limits the possibilities for discovering something new. During streaming live sales, you might be competing with dozens of other people trying to purchase the same item you're interested in. On the other hand, there can be an atmosphere of heightened excitement or frenzy which, if you're not careful, can lead to claiming things you didn't actually want or need. With many small and larger online boutiques offering live

sale streaming and instant shopping, I recommend finding social media vendors that match your own energy levels, values, and aesthetic, and from whom you feel really good about purchasing.

ROCKHOUNDING

There is something truly magical about being the one to unearth a crystal. In the same way that gardening can reconnect you to the land, the elements, the spirit of the plants to which you tend, and the reciprocal relationship between humans and nature, in my opinion, so too does rockhounding when done with respect for the Earth and the crystals being mined.

If you are concerned about how your crystals are being sourced, mining your own is the best way to ensure a complete lack

of exploitative labor and low environmental impact. Having said that, please be sure to do your research beforehand. Respect tribal reservation boundaries, ask permission before mining on private property, and learn how to extract stones in a way that is safe both for you and the land from which you mine.

If you're just getting started, there are many small, family-run businesses that allow you, for a fee, to visit their dig sites and keep what you find. You can also reach out to local rockhounding groups in your community for resources on safe digging locations or join local group expeditions. Besides being a lot of fun, knowing that you're the one who found your new crystals, and put in the effort to uncover them, can strengthen the relationship you have both with them and the Earth.

HOW TO SOURCE WITH INTENTION & AWARENESS

As crystal collecting becomes popularized via social media, it can be easy to focus on a crystal's beauty or benefit and forget the sheer amount of work it took to bring that one tumble into your care.

Experts estimate that crystals pass between 5 and 15 pairs of hands before ever reaching us. There are so many opportunities for these stones to provide financial independence and support to each person who lovingly mines, sorts, polishes, carves, and vends them, but in an increasingly demanding and lucrative market, the crystal industry can just as easily turn exploitative.

When working with crystals for energetic or healing purposes, it's imperative to ensure, as far as we are able, that everyone who helped bring the stone into our lives—from the initial miner all the way to the store associate—was treated with respect and adequately compensated for their time, effort, and work.

It's equally important to remember that if the price of a crystal seems too good, or remarkably low, this often means someone, somewhere along the supply chain, is paying the hidden cost. This could be in the form of environmental degradation, labor exploitation, or communities bearing the brunt of unsustainable practices.

In this section, we explore common mining and carving methods in the hope that greater awareness will help us ask the necessary questions to begin shifting the crystal industry into one that supports the well-being of all those who contribute, while still protecting the Earth that births these remarkable stones.

COMMON CRYSTAL MINING PRACTICES

SURFACE MINING METHODS

Surface mining refers to the technique of accessing shallow deposits of gems and metal ore near the surface of the Earth by removing the vegetation, soil, bedrock, and sometimes even entire mountaintops to reach them. Crystal mining typically falls into two of the three main surface mining techniques. It should be noted: many surface mines were not initially dug for crystals and they were instead collected as by-products of the metal ore deposits for which the mine *was* created.

Open-pit Mining

Open-pit mining involves removing soil and bedrock to create a stepped-sided pit in order to reach the desired minerals below. The pits can vary in size: most crystal pits tend to be smaller, but some ore mines can be miles long, causing drastic changes to the local environment. Typically used for mining metals and gemstones such as diamonds, open-pit mining can produce harmful pollutants depending on the mining process and the material being extracted, which can endanger the miners, as well as the local flora, fauna, and people living nearby. Many nations have regulations in place to mitigate the environmental impact, including rehabilitation of the open pit by filling it up with the removed topsoil and planting vegetation, but recovery can take decades.

Strip Mining

Another environmentally destructive form of surface mining, strip mining requires razing the ground vegetation above a mineral or ore vein, then digging wide, shallow trenches to access the deposits. Once depleted, the leftover rock waste, or "tailings," is placed back into the emptied pit and covered up while moving onto the next strip to be dug. While ore mining often creates chemical exposure hazards due to the treatments necessary to strip the rock of its metals, crystal mining typically doesn't involve this process. Reclamation methods upon depletion of a strip mine can range from filling the hole to creating an artificial lake, planting native plants to rehabilitate the land, or the creation of parks.

UNDERGROUND MINING

In underground mining, varying sized tunnels and chambers are carved down into the earth or into mountain or cliff sides in order to access the metals, ore, and gemstones beneath the Earth's surface. This method can pose risks to workers due to potential cave-ins or structural instability in the surrounding area, but in many ways underground mining is far less harmful to the environment than surface mining as only a small percentage of vegetation needs to be cleared. Although there are numerous types of underground mines, the three most common for crystal extraction are:

Tunneling

One of the most common techniques for crystal mining, a tunnel is built from the surface directly to the vein of gem-bearing hardrock, which is then extended to further tunnels or caverns. The crystals are mined by blasting, drilling, or using

◄ An example of an open-pit iron ore mine in the Amazon rainforest, Para, Brazil. The aerial perspective allows one to see the impact large-scale mines can have on the local ecology.

pickaxes to retrieve them from the surrounding rock. As tunneling doesn't typically require large areas of topographical upheaval, it is the least environmentally impactful of larger mining operations, but mines can vary widely in terms of safety precautions and in responsible waste management and rock disposal.

Chambering

Chambering refers to a vertical shaft that is burrowed into the hardrock next to the crystal or ore vein, and from which tunnels are then drilled and blasted into the vein at different depths from the surface. The gemstones, crystals, or minerals are then mined and brought back to the surface via the vertical shaft. This method is, again, less impactful than open-pit mining, but can still introduce waste pollution into the surrounding environment if not managed carefully.

Room and Pillar

More commonly used for metal or coal extraction, this method of mining can be used to extract minerals that are embedded horizontally in the bedrock. Parallel tunnels are blasted into the ore or stone to create rooms, while large "pillars" of the material are left in place to support the earth above and prevent collapse. This maximizes how much ore or crystal can be extracted, while maintaining the stability of the mountain or strata above the mine. As with the other two underground mining techniques, each mine can vary greatly in terms of its effect on the surrounding ecosystem.

ALLUVIAL DIGGING

Considerably less invasive than either surface or underground mining, alluvial digging involves mining rivers, lakes, and other bodies of water for precious metals and popular crystals such as agates, jaspers, garnets, and amethysts, and even precious stones like ruby or opal.

Placer Mining

Bringing to mind the panning gold-rushers of the 1840s, placer mining involves sifting for gemstones, crystals, or metal from the waters and sediments of a river, lake, or even sea using flat pans, woven baskets, rockers, or filters. For example, a miner fills their pan with water (or sediment) and swirls or shakes it to separate the denser materials and remove rocks. Generally low-impact, panning can create instability in water systems if the floor of the river or lake is disturbed or dredged.

Dry Digging

Dry digging is when miners divert a stream, creek, or river in order to create a dry portion of the original riverbed where they can sift through and gather gemstones, crystals, or metal nuggets. While the greater ecological damage is minimal, this can vary depending on the length of the diverting canal and how much care is taken to minimize the impact on the plants and animals living in the river.

ARTISANAL MINING

Most of the above mining methods (with the exception of river panning and alluvial digging) are employed solely by company-owned operations that can afford to dig large, open pits or room and pillar mines. Yet over 90 percent of the world's crystals and gemstones are mined by small-scale, independent artisanal miners, or ASM. In many developing countries, ASM is one of the main ways of earning an income, with rural families often splitting their time seasonally between agriculture and mining. Many artisanal miners work independently, but some create co-ops to help enforce safety standards and share resources at the local level.

Hand-mining

This practice involves collecting loose, or mining shallowly buried, crystals, typically without disturbing the ecosystem in which they're found. A relatively non-invasive method that is performed only with hand tools, hand-mining limits the ability to excavate compared with machine-powered tools. ASM is generally undertaken by individuals or small groups, making it a low-impact method of crystal mining. Unfortunately, as there is little to no oversight or regulation, there is no guarantee of safety conditions or age restrictions for the practice.

"Lunch-Pail" Mining

This term is used to describe miners who collect crystals opportunistically while working in other industries. Often, to supplement their income, these miners will sell the crystals they find while excavating metal ore. While it can be beneficial for the miners, who are often underpaid, it can contribute to safety issues as they search for stones in unsanctioned parts of a mine, or past hours of operation when others wouldn't be around to help if a dangerous situation arose.

TYPES OF CARVERS

Individual/Family

Small-scale carvers work independently or with extended family, often preserving traditions going back generations. These carvers maintain a deep connection to the local stone, and generally take great pride in their craftsmanship. On the other hand, many individual carvers do so in their own backyards, without the necessary equipment to prevent accidental injury or avoid silicosis (a lung condition caused by breathing crystal dust). Even so, sourcing directly from individual or family operations ensures income and autonomy for these carvers, and helps keep artisan traditions alive.

Co-ops

Co-operative carvers and artisans work collectively, sharing profits and resources such as carving materials, machinery, and safety equipment. This model fosters a sense of community as it trains new generations. It also provides stable livelihoods for those involved because it strengthens the bargaining power with mines from which they source stone and the brokers that purchase the carvers' inventory for the worldwide market. While co-ops tend to lack oversight, they ultimately contribute positively to—and in some cases completely sustain—local economies.

Factories

Larger operations employ skilled workers in factories for mass production. While this can ensure better safety equipment and decent employment opportunities, many parts of the world do not enforce fair wages, age restrictions, or safe working conditions, so due diligence is vital. Many factories also try to undercut the market by buying out mines in other countries, providing little material left for local carvers who depend on their native resources to provide for both their families and communities. When in doubt, try to purchase from regional factories that source stone found nearby.

Brokers

Brokers play a pivotal role in the crystal industry by connecting crystal manufacturers with customers, often purchasing raw crystals directly from mines, carved stones from individuals, co-ops, and factories, and then exporting the material to buyers abroad. Some may be small, but many operate on a large scale, with hundreds of thousands of kilos exported at a time. While brokers facilitate the flow of crystals from source to market, shifting regulations from country to country means it is essential to choose those who prioritize ethical sourcing and uphold responsible and humane business practices.

CONCLUSION

You may notice there is a lot of gray area—and it's true. There is no governing body or trade council in this industry to determine whether how something is mined or where it was carved is considered ethical or not. Buying from artisanal miners and carvers means supporting the local community, but there's no way to guarantee safety conditions. Buying from a factory in a country with strong government regulations to protect employees may still contribute to buying out material from underneath local communities in other parts of the world. And tracing a stone to a particular mine to ensure environmentally friendly practices is next to impossible unless you already know the mine from which it came.

In a global economy, nothing is ever simple. But the more we know, the better choices we can make. Understanding the origin of our crystals and prioritizing suppliers who uphold sustainability, fair labor practices, and community well-being is essential to shifting the crystal industry to one that supports the livelihoods of miners, artisans, and communities while safeguarding the environment for future generations. Every crystal carries a story, and sourcing with intention can help ensure that story is one of integrity, respect, and care.

CRYSTAL COLLECTIONS

Here we come to the heart of the book. Now that we have a foundational understanding of the methods by which crystals are procured, carved, and made available to the public to purchase, we can turn to the crystals themselves.

Part two is subdivided into four main sections, each addressing a different focus for growing our crystal collection. For those of you who may be new to the crystal community, we commence with my top ten crystals to jump-start your collection (*Collecting Crystals by Numbers*). Next, in *Collecting by Intention*, we move on to those who prefer to augment their collection by chakra or zodiac association, or by metaphysical benefit (e.g. for sleep, memory, or creativity). For those more geologically minded, the *Collecting by Type* section focuses on mineralogical families, and dives more thoroughly into the science behind each stone. Finally, in *Collecting by Unique Feature*, we showcase the prized crystal features, inclusions, and formations that are highly sought after by seasoned and discerning collectors.

Whether you choose to center your collection around beauty, spiritual associations, geology, formations, features, or a combination of all the above, my hope is the following pages will serve to inform and inspire you.

COLLECTING CRYSTALS BY NUMBERS

When we first begin our crystal journey, it can feel overwhelming. There are over 5,000 minerals on our incredible planet, with new ones being discovered every year. How do you know where to even start? When asked, I always recommend to go with the crystals that attract you, fascinate you, or just feel good in your hand. Although, there is something to be said for having a starter guide.

The 10 crystals in this beginner's collection may be commonly available, but they are anything but basic. Covering almost all your energetic bases, these crystals are staples that, in my opinion, every crystal connoisseur would benefit from having in their collection.

1 CLEAR QUARTZ

Intention Holding. Energy Amplification. Piezoelectric.

Known as "The Master Crystal," clear quartz is found in almost every country on Earth, and is well known for its ability to hold and transmit any energy.

STONE FAMILY: Quartz
MOHS HARDNESS: 7
CHAKRA: Crown/All

What makes clear quartz so special is its metaphysical *and* scientific properties: it can hold very precise frequencies once programmed and is piezoelectric, meaning it can produce energy (electricity) when the quartz is placed under mechanical stress. This ability to create energy and transmit frequencies makes it a valuable component in watches, computers, televisions, and even satellites, as well as for the lenses in microscopes, telescopes, and lasers. Nowadays, most clear quartz crystals for technology and equipment are grown in laboratories, but our use of natural clear quartz dates back almost 30,000 years. Excavations at many ancient burial sites have unearthed clear quartz amulets, believed to be talismans for the afterlife. Our fascination with this stone hasn't diminished, and for thousands of years it has been carved into tools, beads and jewelry, glassware, religious artifacts, and even just used as a decorative item.

Metaphysically, clear quartz's properties align with its scientific ones: as a Master Crystal, the magic of quartz lies in its ability to hold frequencies—from another crystal, an energetic source, or a specific programmed intention—and transmit that frequency into the Universe. Clear quartz can take the place of almost any other stone and is a powerful amplifier for crystal grids. Programming a quartz crystal with an intention and then keeping it close can help you manifest that intention into reality, while natural points or carved wands are powerful tools for focusing energy during rituals.

2 AMETHYST

Intuition. Self-awareness. Temperance.

Amethyst is one of the most versatile, popular, and beloved crystals. Gently protective, amethyst shows what is aligned for us, while its soothing energy will bring a feeling of calm to any living space.

STONE FAMILY: Quartz
MOHS HARDNESS: 7
CHAKRA: Third Eye

Amethyst takes its name from the ancient Greek *amethystos*, meaning "not intoxicated." Legend has it that Dionysus, the Greek god of wine, transformed an innocent woman into clear crystal. Instantly remorseful, he emptied his cup of wine upon the stone, staining it purple as a pledge to never again lose his temper while inebriated. Although the ancient Greeks believed amethyst could prevent intoxication, it is now understood to ease tempers and support the release of unaligned and harmful habits by encouraging self-awareness. A crystal of the Third Eye chakra, amethyst awakens intuition and is gently protective. It opens our minds to the spiritual nature of life, helping us return to the present moment when feeling harried, reactive, or triggered.

Ranging in hue from lavender, to a pinkish-plum, to the juiciest dark purple, the color of amethyst is derived from traces of iron within quartz that was subjected to natural radiation as it formed. Found around the world, from Siberia to Mexico, amethyst can grow into a variety of different formations, depending on the environment. It is often found as clusters, geodes, high-grade saturated hexagonal points, large microcrystalline deposits (like chevron amethyst), and even as "bouquets" of wands, such as Bahia amethyst. The price range for amethyst can vary widely according to its locality and grade, with the highest caliber stones faceted for jewelry and large geode "churches" reserved for home decor. It is readily available at most stores and gem shows.

3 ROSE QUARTZ

Divine Love. Romantic Love.
Familial Love. Self-love.

The quintessential stone of love, rose quartz resonates with the frequencies of Universal Love, within which every aspect of this all-important emotion is encompassed.

STONE FAMILY: Quartz
MOHS HARDNESS: 7
CHAKRA: Heart

While other stones might delve into the specifics of Heart chakra healing, rose quartz is the crystal to turn to when we wish to call more love into our lives: helping us connect with others more authentically, find compassion for each other, heal a broken heart, find romantic partners, repair relationship wounds, and, most importantly of all, connect to and love ourselves, deeply and fully. Divine and Universal Love have no conditions and no limitations, and rose quartz helps us break free from the societal conditioning that says we aren't enough and don't deserve to be loved exactly as we are in each moment. This gentle pink stone reminds us that we are always enough, and if the Universe can love us in our entirety, then others can and will too.

For such an important stone, it's no surprise that rose quartz is found on every inhabited continent. While rare crystal specimens can be found in certain areas of Brazil, rose quartz typically grows as microcrystalline boulders, which are left raw or can be carved or polished into just about any shape. Rose quartz usually ranges from a pale glassy blush to deep bubble-gum shades, all thanks to the presence of dididumortierite (microscopically tiny, pink fibers). Rose quartz pairs well with almost any crystal, and is a perfect stone to wear as jewelry, keep by the bed, or utilize in ritual baths.

4 BLACK TOURMALINE

Grounding. Mental, Emotional, and Spiritual Protection. Physical Safety.

Also known as schorl, people turn to this crystal most often when they are feeling unsteady or unsafe. It is one of the most accessible and preeminent of the Root chakra crystals.

STONE FAMILY: Tourmaline
MOHS HARDNESS: 7-7.5
CHAKRA: Root

Known for its ability to form an impenetrable energetic shield around us, black tourmaline protects against unaligned or denser energies. When we are feeling untethered, flighty, or emotionally dissociated, this guardian crystal can help us return to our bodies, infusing us with feelings of security. A powerful grounding stone, black tourmaline supports the deep reconnection of our Root (or base) chakra to the Earth's energetic field, and safely balances out the intensity of high-frequency stones like moldavite or Herkimer diamond.

Typically inexpensive (except for notable terminated specimens), black tourmaline is found throughout the world. Most crystal stores carry black tourmaline in its raw form, from tiny pieces all the way up to large logs. While this can be a strong or dense stone, it is prone to chipping or flaking due to imperfections in the growth patterns and inclusions such as mica or quartz. It can occasionally be tumbled, or carved into towers or spheres if the stone is dense enough. Black tourmaline is perfect to use during meditation in order to ground yourself, keep in the car or at home (especially near entryways), or wear as jewelry to invoke its protective qualities throughout the day.

5 SELENITE

Clearing. Purifying. Elevated Vibration.
Historically Used to Make Beads and Jewelry

Like the crystalline version of sacred smoke, selenite raises the frequency of whatever it is near, purifying the energy of a space, the auras of those close by, and even fellow crystals.

STONE FAMILY: Gypsum
MOHS HARDNESS: 2
CHAKRA: Crown

Selenite is named after Selene, the Greek goddess of the Moon, as a result of its luminous glow which resembles moonlight. It is a stone of cleansing and purification.

The crystallized form of gypsum, selenite is an "evaporite," which means the ionic gypsum solution forms crystals as the water evaporates. As a result, selenite is typically found in desert areas such as those in Morocco, the North American Southwest, and Mexico. Pictured here is an opaque fibrous variety known as satin spar, which is the most readily available, easy-to-carve, and least expensive form of selenite, although beautifully clear crystal specimens can also be sourced from Mexico and golden clusters have even been found in Utah.

You can work with selenite in many ways. Place the crystal above or by a door frame to clear the energy coming into the home or on your altar to keep it continually sanctified. If you work with clients, this natural sulfuric salt crystal is also a good choice for easily clearing the space between sessions. Wearing selenite creates a bubble of light around you, helping clear away what is unaligned before it even reaches you. It is also perfect as part of a ritual to cleanse your own energy field: simply hold a piece of selenite and imagine "erasing" attachments and blockages in your aura, feeling them dissolve in the light of selenite's vibrational field. Note: As an evaporite, exposure to water can reverse the process over time, so keep selenite away from humidity and the elements.

6 GREEN AVENTURINE

Luck. Abundance and Prosperity. Growth. Health.

Sparkling and verdant, green aventurine—historically used to make beads, jewelry, and to decorate statues of deities—has been associated with wealth and well-being for millennia.

STONE FAMILY: Quartz
MOHS HARDNESS: 7
CHAKRA: Heart

Considered the luckiest of all stones, green aventurine invites opportunity, prosperity, and health through its frequency of joy-filled growth and abundance. It infuses our energy field with optimism and gratitude, reminding us of all the ways that we're already wealthy and making it easier to magnetize aligned abundance to ourselves. Associated with the miraculous regeneration of the natural world, green aventurine also supports physical health and is excellent to work with when people, plants, or animals need to heal, mend, or recuperate.

Green aventurine's iridescent sparkles and leafy hue come from chrome-bearing mica flakes known as fuchsite, distributed throughout the quartz, which catch and reflect the light in a prismatic display. A relatively inexpensive crystal, green aventurine is readily available and commonly found in all crystal stores. The deeper the color, the more saturated the quartz is with fuchsite, with vivid green deposits often trade named "Green Strawberry Quartz." A microcrystalline member of the silicate family, green aventurine is mined from veins and pockets all over the world, and then carved into any shape imaginable, including ornamental figurines, towers, bowls, beads and jewelry, or lucky talismans. Green aventurine is water-safe, making it a perfect addition to any garden or container to boost the health and growing potential of plants. It can also be used in crystal grids, stored in a wallet/purse, or worn to invite luck, prosperity, and health into our lives.

7 CITRINE

Wealth. Manifestation. Self-worth.

Resonating with our Solar Plexus chakra,
the center of self, citrine invites abundance
by reminding us of our own worth.

STONE FAMILY: Quartz
MOHS HARDNESS: 7
CHAKRA: Solar Plexus

Golden citrine reflects the riches it is fabled to bring. Citrine asks us to remember that we are divine, unique, and powerful beings. We are worthy of whatever aligned wealth means to us and of enjoying the life of our dreams. But if we don't fully believe such abundance is possible or that we're worthy of prosperity, it is difficult for the Universe to co-create that life with us.

Citrine's inherent warmth and energy can help us shift into a more positive mindset and asks us to focus on how we're already wealthy rather than on what we lack. By raising our vibration, emanating gratitude, and embodying the certainty that we're worthy, we can begin to magnetize this actuality into our lives. Citrine helps us gain and maintain wealth, while simultaneously instilling generosity within us.

Some ways to work with this crystal include making a manifestation crystal grid or creating a money bag with a tumbled citrine and other stones that represent abundance to you. If Feng Shui resonates with you, keep citrine in the wealth corner of your home or business, or place this water-safe crystal at the base of a houseplant to create a "money tree."

Citrine tends to grow in points or cathedral formations, usually cut along the base to form towers, while rarer, larger crystals can be carved. It's sometimes found in areas that also produce smoky quartz; when these pockets overlap a darker hued "smoky citrine" is produced. Much of the "citrine" for sale is amethyst turned orange with high heat or treated lemon quartz. Real citrine has a golden or honey-toned hue.

8 CARNELIAN

Artistic Creativity. Inspiration.
Passion. Fertility. Creation.

Carnelian reminds us that the passions of our lives, in whatever form they take, add depth and color to the realities of our day and, in the end, will be what make our lives a beautiful story worth telling.

STONE FAMILY: Chalcedony
MOHS HARDNESS: 7
CHAKRA: Sacral

Many people are passionate about carnelian, which isn't surprising since it's a stone for inspiring passion. A muse for any type of creative art, carnelian reconnects us with pure Source, showing us how to tap into what is waiting to be born through us, whether that be a novel, a song, a painting, or even a new business idea. Equally adept at inspiring physical passion, carnelian is famous for its ability to revitalize our desires, being particularly supportive when we are trying to conceive new life. Carnelian asks us to sit with our desires instead of rejecting them: What are they trying to tell us? How big or small do we want our lives to be? What do we wish to create in the time we have?

A red-banded variety of agate, carnelian typically hails from Brazil, India, Egypt, Uruguay, or Madagascar. Microcrystalline carnelian has been used for amulets since ancient times, but is today carved into a variety of shapes, including hearts, towers, flames, or, for those interested in its fertility benefits, eggs or anatomical figurines.

As carnelian can have both creative or physical properties, it is best used with clear intention. To enhance physical passion, keep carnelian near or under the bed. To balance hormones, ease menstrual cramping, or increase the chance of conceiving, lay carnelian on your pelvis while meditating, or keep it on your nightstand. I keep carnelian on my desk to aid creative flow, but it can also be kept with your oil paints, guitar case, or dance bag. Carnelian reminds us that inspiration and passion are always there to enhance life.

9 SODALITE

Writing. Communication of Thoughts and Concepts. Insight. Focus. Cognitive Function.

Exuding an energy that is steadying, balanced, and nuanced, Sodalite assists in discernment, encourages a clear perspective, and creates space for us to recognize our own truth.

STONE FAMILY: Sodalite
MOHS HARDNESS: 5.5-6
CHAKRA: Throat, Third Eye

Called the "Writer's Stone," "Poet's Stone," and "Stone of Truth," it's no wonder deep blue sodalite has become a favorite since its recognition in 1811. Sodalite is a crystal of intellectual understanding and thoughtful expression, helping us take all the information we have learned, all the observations we have made, all the truths bubbling within, and coalesce them into words. A stone of poetry, sodalite supports the translation of concepts, however heartfelt, however complex, into something that can be understood by those around us. Whether we merely wish to communicate clearly or are endeavoring to paint the world anew with our writing, sodalite encourages us to allow the words to flow.

To harness the benefits of sodalite, keep this stone where you work or write. Wearing or keeping a small sodalite tumble in your pocket when traveling eases translation and communication. Intellectually stimulating, sodalite is perfect for students to keep on hand in class when they need to absorb a lot of information and equally helpful when writing papers or theses. Geologically the blue variety is only one member of the sodalite group, but it is by far the most common. Traded and utilized as beads by Indigenous communities in South America, sodalite only rose to commercial prominence as an ornamental stone in 1891 when a large deposit was found in Canada. Nowadays, most sodalite is also sourced from the United States, Brazil, Russia, and India.

10 LEPIDOLITE

Calming. Soothing. Anti-anxiety.
Emotional/Mental Balance.

Lepidolite is a soothing and gentle emotional-balancing stone, particularly supportive for calming our nervous system during periods of anxiety, depression, or stress.

STONE FAMILY: Mica
MOHS HARDNESS: 2.5-4
CHAKRA: Third Eye, Crown

For the final stone in this starter collection, I've selected lepidolite, an easy-to-source, purple or pink mica with natural lithium that emanates serenity and balance. Lepidolite is a supportive stone for when we are experiencing stress, anxiety, tension, mood disorders, or insomnia. When our nervous system becomes heightened, either from low-level chronic stress or spiking anxiety, lepidolite steps in to energetically help us down-regulate and shift back into a parasympathetic state of calm awareness. For those of us who have difficulty sleeping due to swirling thoughts or emotions, lepidolite gently absorbs the strain and apprehension of the day, making it easier to fall asleep and dream sweetly.

As a mica, lepidolite can vary greatly in hardness, ranging from fragile layers of pure mica "books" to denser varieties containing "impurities" that allow it to be tumbled, or carved into towers, spheres, or even intricate statues. Lepidolite is often found growing in pegmatites with quartzes, tourmalines, and feldspars, and so works particularly well with crystals from those families, along with other micas.

If you are prone to anxiety, experiencing a stressful situation, or moving through a difficult time, lepidolite is most supportive when worn or kept at hand, and is particularly effective as a worry stone or meditation ally. For insomnia or nightmares, place lepidolite by the bed or under your pillow to facilitate the transition to a more tranquil sleep.

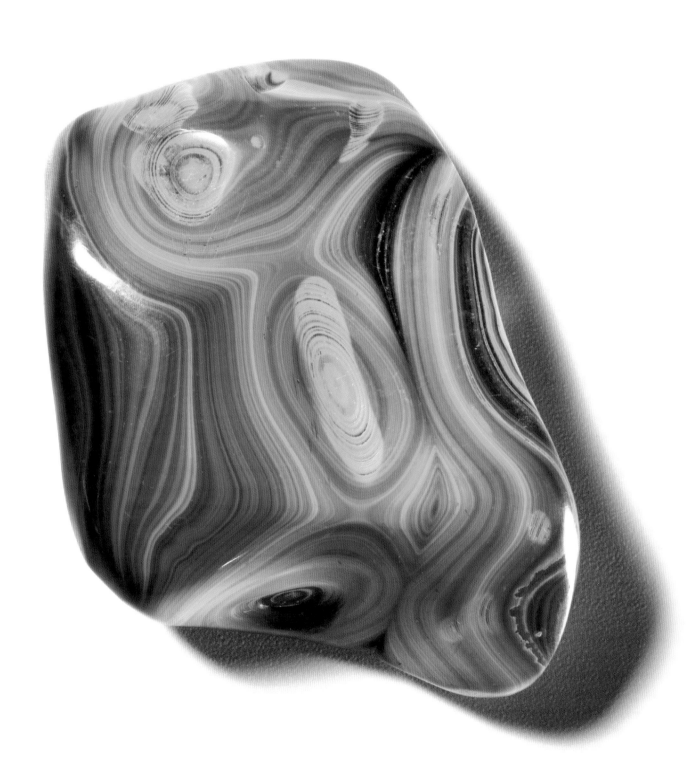

COLLECTING BY INTENTION

How we choose to grow our collection can vary from person to person, but selecting stones based on energy and attributed metaphysical properties has become more and more common, even mainstream, over the past few years. We might seek out supportive stones for a particular need or situation we're currently moving through, or maybe we wish to work with crystals to tap into our ability to manifest a specific result, or encourage a certain way of feeling. The crystals in the Intention Collection on the following pages are the ones I am asked for most often, but they still only offer a small taste of the unlimited possibilities crystals can offer us.

CRYSTALS FOR CHAKRA
Energetically Aligned Stones for the Chakra Centers

Dating back to ancient India, the chakras are a system of energetic centers throughout the body. Each chakra relates to different parts of our physiology, experience, and aspect of spiritual growth. Crystals, like mantras, mudras, yoga poses, and tones, can be utilized to activate, balance, and clear blockages from specific chakras. Illustrated on pages 42–43 *(see corresponding numbers)*.

EARTH STAR CHAKRA
Vasundhara
Location: 3–12in (7½–30cm) beneath the feet
Color: Brown
Mantra: I connect

The Earth Star chakra serves as the grounding point for the entire aura, or etheric body. This energy center tethers us deeply to the heart and consciousness of Gaia (Mother Earth), allowing us to connect to the ley lines and Akashic Records (see page 140), not just of our planet, but the whole of the human collective.

1. Star Aragonite
Star aragonite enhances our ability to tap into the ley lines of the planet and assists in the energetic exchange between the self and the Earth's consciousness.

2. Shaman Stone
Shaman stone strengthens our energetic roots into the Earth, facilitating shamanic journeying, elemental communication, and rebalancing the polarity of the energetic field back to the Schumann Frequency (the dominant resonant frequency of the Earth).

ROOT CHAKRA
Muladhara
Location: Base of the spine (the tailbone)
Color: Red/Black
Mantra: I am

The Root chakra is the center of safety, stability, and groundedness. When we feel our energetic roots reach deep into the earth, we know we are taken care of and that our foundations are strong. When our Root chakra is balanced—in other words, when we know ourselves to be safe—anything becomes possible.

1. Black Tourmaline
Mentally, emotionally, and physically protective, black tourmaline blocks perceived negative energies. Schorl Tourmaline is also one of the most grounding of all stones.

2. Smoky Quartz
Grounding and filtering, smoky quartz transmutes unaligned energies back to the Earth. It also supports physical embodiment and integration of higher frequencies.

3. Hematite
Deeply grounding and detoxifying, hematite supports feelings of safety and is also adept at grounding spiritual energies into the physical realm.

4. Hematoid Quartz
Hematite-included quartz balances, stabilizes, and energizes. It's helpful in overcoming anxiety or fear, and discerning what is a triggered reaction versus a necessary response.

5. Red Calcite
A stone of embodiment that supports an appreciation of our body and experiences as a physical being. It also provides a gentle infusion of *prana* (or *chi*) via the Root chakra.

SACRAL CHAKRA
Svadhishthana
Location: Lower abdomen (about 2in/5cm) below the navel
Color: Orange
Mantra: I feel/I create

The Sacral chakra is the energetic space of creation within the body. Whether we're generating new life, tapping into our artistic creativity, or "birthing" a new endeavor, the Sacral center is fertile ground for all we're capable of creating.

1. Carnelian
A crystal of passion, artistry, inspiration, and fertility, carnelian encourages us to bring forth the life—whether creative, entrepreneurial, or physical—waiting within ourselves.

2. Tangerine Quartz
A stone of curiosity, creativity, and enthusiasm, tangerine quartz releases shame and supports engagement with our passions, whether artistic or corporeal.

3. Vanadinite
Vanadinite opens the space for inspiration and innovation, and provides us with the stamina to complete the projects and artistic endeavors we have begun.

4. Garnet
An embodiment stone, garnet assists us in finding joy in the physical world, as well as security, self-acceptance, and passion within our physical body.

5. Orange Calcite
Orange calcite stimulates playfulness (in children) and healthy sexuality (in adults), and supports the inspiration and fulfillment that can come from having fun.

SOLAR PLEXUS CHAKRA
Manipura
Location: Upper abdomen (stomach)
Color: Yellow/Gold
Mantra: I do

The Solar Plexus is the seat of our willpower, motivation, confidence, and sense of self-worth. This center empowers us to take action, manifest the world we wish to see, and remember how unique, important, and valuable we are. When in alignment, the actions we take and the light we shine can't help but benefit and catalyze others.

1. Pyrite
A literal and energetic "fire starter," pyrite shows us how to manifest through sparks of personal willpower and purposeful action. Being protective, pyrite also inspires strength and confidence.

2. Citrine
Citrine helps magnetize wealth and abundance through the expansion of our self-worth. It instills self-confidence and joy.

3. Tiger's Eye
A crystal of energetic strength, vitality, and abundance, tiger's eye balances the mind and the will through discernment, practicality, and enlightened action.

4. Golden Healer
A master healer, this uncommon variety of hematoid quartz unlocks our divine innate ability to heal ourselves physically and energetically.

5. Honey Calcite
Inspiring confidence and persistence, honey calcite clears blockages and infuses energy into this chakra. Unites the mental clarity and focused will needed to complete goals.

HEART CHAKRA
Anahata
Location: Center of the chest
Color: Green/Pink
Mantra: I love

The Heart is known to be the most powerful energetic center in the body, where the lower and upper chakras merge, and through which we ultimately connect to ourselves and to each other. The energy of the Heart is suffused with Love: for when we think, express, and act with compassion and love, we heal and expand ourselves and others.

1. Rose Quartz
The ultimate Heart chakra stone that encompasses love in all its myriad forms. Rose quartz realigns heart-centered frequencies, inviting and inspiring compassion and self-love.

2. Pink Opal
A stone of emotional healing and peace, heart-calming pink opal eases loneliness and is supportive in recovering from heartbreak.

3. Green Aventurine
Inviting abundance and prosperity, green aventurine is considered the luckiest of stones, while also supporting the physical health and vitality of humans, animals, and plants.

4. Chrysoprase
Chrysoprase connects with the renewing energy of nature, and is associated with new beginnings, regeneration, joy, emotional growth, and forgiveness.

5. Mangano Calcite
A crystal of empathy, compassion, and loving boundaries, mangano calcite invites deep heart healing, and encourages connection, emotional wholeness, and recovery from grief.

THROAT CHAKRA
Vishuddha
Location: Throat
Color: Blue
Mantra: I speak

Placed midway between the Third Eye and Heart chakras, it is through the throat that we articulate our thoughts and convey our emotions. This is the center responsible for communication, language, and music, enabling us to create ripples within the energetic fabric of the world by fully expressing our truest selves.

1. Aquamarine
Enhancing clear and healthy communication, aquamarine cools tempers and soothes emotional upheavals, helping us flow in alignment with life.

2. Amazonite
A crystal of harmony and courage, amazonite supports the realization of Inner Truth, honest and heartfelt communication, and the ability to listen when others share their truth.

3. Turquoise
Steadying and protective, turquoise encourages the sharing and receiving of wisdom, as well as spiritual and emotional expansion through communication.

4. Chrysocolla
Compassionate and creative, chrysocolla supports the expression and communication of emotions through music, stories, poetry, movement, and art.

5. Larimar
Serene yet transformative, larimar washes away blockages in the Throat chakra and helps us to effectively inform others of our needs and boundaries.

THIRD EYE CHAKRA
Ajna
Location: The pineal gland, between and above the eyes
Color: Indigo/Violet
Mantra: I see

Also known as the Brow chakra, this is the dualistic seat of analysis and intuition, conscious thought and unconscious perception. It is the center of Self-awareness. Through the mind we think, process, remember, and plan, but it is through our "inner eye" that we become aware of the energetic world beyond the physical.

1. Amethyst
A calming, purifying, and protective stone, amethyst promotes self-awareness, easing the release of harmful habits and patterns that stand in the way of spiritual growth.

2. Labradorite
Labradorite awakens our innate spiritual gifts and magnetizes synchronicities, heightening the awareness of magic in everyday life.

3. Iolite
Iolite enhances intuition and facilitates access to the spiritual realms, assisting in spiritual and shamanic journeys, astral projection, and past-life regression.

4. Azurite
Azurite stimulates both the spiritual and pragmatic parts of the mind, deepening intuition practices and balancing those with intellectual wisdom.

5. Fluorite
Supporting both intuition and mental clarity, fluorite clears the mind of confusion and aids analytical thought, decision-making, and memory retention.

CROWN CHAKRA
Sahasrara
Location: Top of the head
Color: Violet/White/Clear
Mantra: I know/I understand

The seventh of the embodied chakras, the Crown is the center of higher consciousness, spirituality, and enlightenment, through which Source energy flows into our physical vessels. Whether we are meditating, dreaming, or connecting to guides, the Crown chakra is where we find objectivity, and experience an inner sense of knowing.

1. Clear Quartz
The Master Crystal, clear quartz holds information and amplifies energy, including that of purposely programmed intentions or even other stones.

2. Moonstone
A protective stone of intuition, insight, and magic, moonstone in any color is also supportive of dreamwork, self-discovery, and embracing the goddess within us all.

3. Selenite
Selenite is purifying, clearing energetic blockages and auric debris. Silvery selenite supports the infusion of Light Energy into the body and the space around us.

4. Apophyllite
A meditation aid, apophyllite lifts the vibration of our energetic field, facilitating connection to guides, angels, and other dimensions.

5. Howlite
A calming and soothing stone, howlite quiets racing thoughts and turbulent emotions, offering space to simply breathe and rest.

SOUL STAR

Vyapini

Location: 3–12in (7½–30cm) above the head
Color: Clear/White
Mantra: I transcend

The Soul Star chakra serves as the tether between us and Universal Consciousness. Representing the gateway to the Divine and our connection to the Higher Self, this is the center of transcendence beyond this lifetime, allowing us to tap into the deep wisdom we always carry with us at the soul level.

1. Herkimer Diamond
One of the highest vibrational forms of quartz, purifying Herkimer diamonds amplify high-frequencied divine energy and support visions, rapid ascension, and spiritual healing.

2. Astrophyllite
Astrophyllite catalyzes realignment with our true path and remembrance of our purpose in this lifetime. It is a powerful aid in astral travel and the embodiment of the Higher Self.

5

2

4

3

1

Throat Chakra

5

2

3

4

1

Solar Plexus Chakra

5

4

1

3

5

2

Root Chakra

3

1

2

5

4

Heart Chakra

5
2
3
4
4
1

Crown Chakra

2
1
2

Soul Star Chakra

3
2
5
4
1

Sacral Chakra

5
5
1
2
4
3

Third Eye Chakra

1
2
2

Earth Star Chakra

CRYSTALS BY ZODIAC

One of the questions most often asked in my store is "What's a good crystal for ____ sign?"

Almost everyone nowadays knows at least a little about astrology. Dating apps ask for our signs, while checking horoscopes and transits has practically become mainstream. I always remind my customers and clients when asked this question: we are more than just our sun sign. Don't limit yourself. We have an entire beautiful natal chart full of planets, nodes, and more, that each contributes to our unique blueprint. Crystals are an energetic yet physical way to enhance or balance the attributes of any sign in our chart, as well as a simple but meaningful method of tuning into and harnessing the energies of its specific season throughout the year. The stones featured here are by no means an exhaustive list, but each one has metaphysical properties that align with the strengths and characteristics of the twelve zodiac signs.

◄ While your birthdate is an easy way to deduce your sun sign, a full natal chart reveals the placements of all the planets that made up the celestial map when you were born.

ARIES
March 21–April 19

Associations: Courageous, Passionate, Independent, Self-Willed, Impatient

Red Jasper
Red jasper harnesses Aries' energy of physical vitality, along with the passion and determination to forge ahead in pursuit of one's desires.

Pyrite
Pyrite enhances the initiatory fire within Aries, the spark that can turn into a flame through sheer willpower and drive. Dissolving insecurities, pyrite boosts confidence and provides the courage needed to take action.

TAURUS
April 20–May 20

Associations: Industrious, Stable, Prosperous, Epicurean, Stubborn

Peridot
Peridot overflows with the Taurean spirit of a life thoroughly enjoyed and richly lived. Embodying the joy-filled abundance that comes from reaping the rewards of our efforts, peridot exudes the vibration of gratitude, satisfaction, and generosity.

Green Aventurine
Green aventurine is an earth-energied crystal that taps into Taurus's natural inclination to magnetize prosperity and well-being.

GEMINI
May 21–June 20

Associations: Adaptable, Quick-Witted, Sociable, Curious, Flighty

Sodalite
Sodalite exemplifies Gemini's natural aptitude for intellectual wit, curiosity, impactful writing, and sociable conversation, while also steadying this sign's sometimes flighty nature.

Blue Lace Agate
Aligned with Gemini's skill in thoughtful, accurate, and articulate communication, blue lace agate is a crystal of airy spaciousness and also a calming presence for the lighthearted twins to balance out their consistent need for freedom and stimulation.

CANCER
June 21–July 22

Associations: Nurturing, Intuitive, Caring, Expressive, Insecure

Opalized Ammonite
Ancient watery ammonite supports Cancer in its desire to build a home that feels safe, nurturing, and loved. Ammonite also represents present-moment living, helping Cancer release worries from the past and move more resolutely toward the future.

Moonstone
Ruled by the Moon, Cancer's association with moonstone is clear. Protective moonstone's night-aligned feminine nature amplifies Cancer's intuition, emotional intelligence, and nurturing spirit.

LEO
July 23–August 22

Associations: Regal, Generous, Playful, Warm, Proud

Tiger's Eye
Tiger's eye enhances the innate power and strength of Leo while balancing this sign's pride with perspective. Offering clarity and discernment, tiger's eye supports taking aligned action that not only benefits oneself, but also everyone else.

Sunstone
Radiating with the benevolent warmth of the Sun—Leo's ruling planet—sunstone embodies the attributes of joy, regality, and leadership commonly associated with Leo.

VIRGO
August 23–September 22

Associations: Organized, Practical, Loving, Hardworking, Critical

Flower Agate
Flower agate typifies the blossoming nature of earthen Virgo when the energies of love and occupation meet. Practical yet optimistic, flower agate supports Virgo's need to plant seeds and watch them grow without judgment.

Blue Sapphire
Blue sapphire encapsulates Virgo's natural talent for analytical thought and critical reasoning. A stone of integrity, blue sapphire taps into the kindness, honesty, and conscientiousness for which Virgo is famous.

LIBRA
September 23 - October 22

Associations: Diplomatic, Fair, Accommodating, Co-operative, Indecisive

Blue Topaz
Emanating the energy of balance, blue topaz taps into Libra's skill for diplomatic dialogue, co-operation, seeing other points of view beyond our own, and forming connections with others. Dissolving reactive tempers, blue topaz supports clear thinking, as well as a wise and just mindset.

Blue Kyanite
A peaceful crystal of connection, blue kyanite accentuates the Libran gifts of harmony, communication, and co-operation, while also encouraging this sometimes conflict-avoidant sign to more easily express their own truth.

SCORPIO
October 23 - November 21

Associations:
Magnetic, Resilient, Sensitive, Passionate, Focused

Obsidian
Formed of volcanic glass, black-mirrored obsidian is a stone of protection, clarity, and magic. Although it can be as sharp as Scorpio's sting, obsidian enhances this sign's powers of perception and awareness, while also repelling what makes Scorpio feel unsafe.

Rhodochrosite
Rhodochrosite, a crystal of Self-love and emotional healing, exemplifies the innate courage of Scorpio to feel deeply—even after being wounded or misunderstood—and amplifies the powerful resiliency of this sign.

SAGITTARIUS
November 22 - December 21

Associations:
Adventurous, Philosophical, Knowledgeable, Independent, Outspoken

Lapis Lazuli
Aligned with Jupiter, the ruling planet of the archer, lapis lazuli is a stone of leaders and divine connection. Lapis supports the deep inner journey during which Sagittarius thrives, as well as teaching discernment in how best to communicate the wisdom one has to share.

Labradorite
Flashing labradorite evokes Sagittarius's innermost purpose. A stone of hidden alchemy, rainbow labradorite invites one to find the hidden meaning of life as it magnetizes synchronicities and reveals the mystery and magic in the everyday.

CAPRICORN
December 22–January 19

Associations: Ambitious, Self-Reliant, Prudent, Disciplined, Tenacious

Black Onyx
Grounding black onyx is supportive of the patient but ever tenacious Capricorn, and exemplifies the inner strength, resilience, and decisiveness of this ambitious earth sign.

Bronzite
A stone of inner stability, bronzite supports the goat's ability to navigate rocky or challenging situations with confidence and discipline. A stone of prudence and resourcefulness, bronzite eases Capricorn's tendency to condescend, and see instead the value that everyone brings to the table.

AQUARIUS
January 20–February 18

Associations: Progressive, Individualistic, Idealistic, Humanitarian, Intelligent

Amethyst
Clarifying amethyst balances out the dual nature of Aquarius's individual and humanitarian sides through self-awareness. By accepting the entirety of oneself and focusing on the work within—the microcosm—one creates ripples that affect the macrocosm of the whole world, ultimately evolving humanity.

Turquoise
Turquoise enhances the qualities of knowledge, communication, spiritual expansion, and wholeness of the self and human collective that are the hallmarks of progressive Aquarius.

PISCES
February 19–March 20

Associations: Dreamy, Spiritual, Empathetic, Imaginative, Emotional

Larimar
Larimar is a feminine-energied water elemental stone, and like Pisces, is famed for the emotional wisdom it carries. A soothing crystal, larimar supports spiritual exploration, self-expression, and honest communication.

Aquamarine
Named for the sea, aquamarine allows Pisces to swim safely in the ebb and flow of their emotional tides, without losing themselves. Aquamarine helps the sensitive fish self-regulate and communicate more directly, without losing any of their natural empathy or compassion.

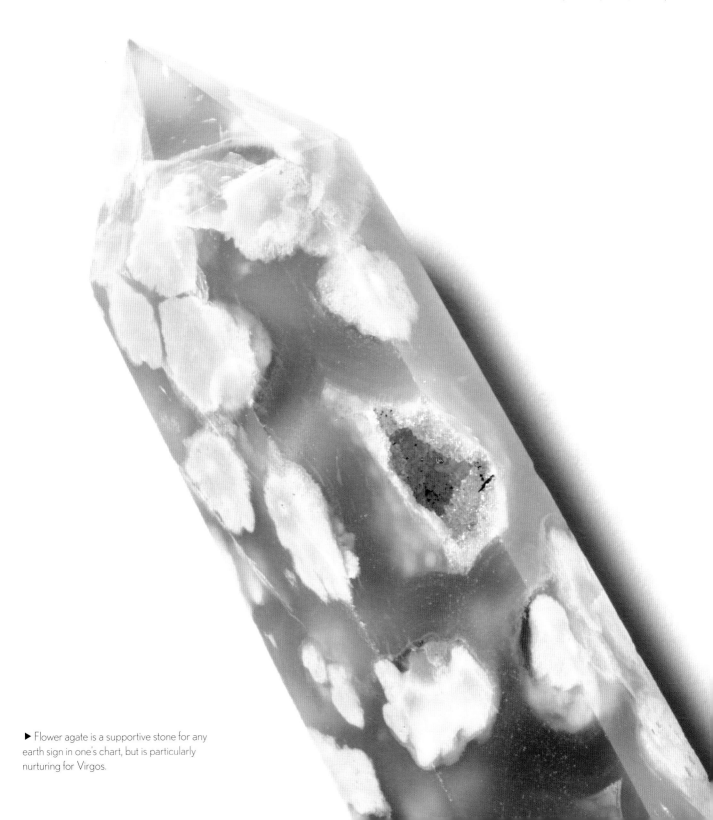

▶ Flower agate is a supportive stone for any
earth sign in one's chart, but is particularly
nurturing for Virgos.

CRYSTALS FOR LOVE

It is only human to crave love. The stages of life are defined by it: parental love, the acceptance of friends, romantic love, and the trust of those we care for. It's through self-love we heal and grow. These stones are gentle and supportive allies, reminding us love truly is the foundation of all.

When I move through the world with an open heart, love surrounds me wherever I go.

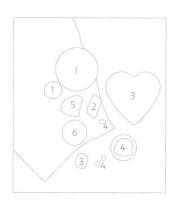

1. ROSE QUARTZ

Nothing encapsulates the undiluted energy of Love more than rose quartz. Keep this crystal near to strengthen the frequencies of your heart, to make finding compassion for others a little easier, as a talisman to call in more love to your life, or as a crystalline support system when struggling to fully love and accept yourself.

2. KUNZITE

Kunzite is a Divine Mothering crystal. For those welcoming new life, kunzite helps forge the connection between parent and child, eases post-partum struggles, and facilitates the transition from One to Family. For those of us who did not receive all the love a child needs in our formative years, kunzite can step in to soothe and support the healing of those core wounds, and release the blocks we've set around our hearts, so we can fully give and receive love as adults.

3. MANGANO CALCITE

A crystal of compassionate and loving boundaries, mangano calcite shows us how to love ourselves and others healthily. It reminds us to fill our own cup first, as only then can it spill forth to nurture others. This sweet and calming pink calcite is especially supportive for caretakers, healers, or those recovering from grief, helping us find the nourishing joy that lights us up, connect empathetically, and maintain the boundaries that are themselves an act of love.

4. MORGANITE

This pink variety of beryl embodies Divine Love and connection to the loving frequency of Universal Source. When we're feeling scared, hurt, or heartbroken, morganite invites us to zoom out, release judgment, look beyond the words and actions of others, and see the divinity within us all. We are all one, connected and co-creating this life together. Morganite asks us to trust, and remember that the Universe loves us unconditionally.

5. PINK TOURMALINE

Resonating with the Heart chakra, pink tourmaline holds the frequency of kindness, safety, love, and happiness. It heals and balances the emotional body, enabling us to relinquish our need to hold on to past hurts as a form of protection. Pink tourmaline asks us to let go, be vulnerable, open our hearts back up to the possibilities of life, and be amazed when love comes flooding back in.

6. EUDIALYTE

Eudialyte is a stone of Self-love, encouraging us to first turn inward to find the cherishing, acceptance, and certainty we seek, and then bravely follow our hearts and lead with love in every choice we make. Dissolving fear, self-doubt, and confusion, eudialyte inspires us to honor ourselves and our aspirations, beyond what society dictates and beyond the narrative that we only have value if someone else loves us. Eudialyte shows us that just being alive makes us worthy of all our dreams, and our most important relationship is always with ourselves.

CRYSTALS FOR ABUNDANCE & PROSPERITY

Whether we envision great wealth or just wish to meet the needs of our families, we all desire abundance in order to enjoy our most aligned lives. The crystals below invite aligned abundance by showing us that properity is everywhere and we're worthy of everything we truly desire.

I am worthy of my dreams. Co-creating with the Universe brings me abundance.

1. CITRINE
The Law of Attraction states that the Universe meets us exactly where we are. Citrine welcomes abundance into our lives by reminding us just how much we are truly worth. When we value ourselves as Divine Beings, worthy of being supported and worthy of all the abundance we can possibly imagine, the Universe cannot help but respond in kind.

2. PYRITE
Pyrite is associated with the inner fire of our will. Encouraging us to make those choices and take those actions, pyrite shows us how, by doing, we are capable of changing the world around us into one of fulfillment and financial stability.

3. GREEN JADE
Jade has traditionally represented good luck, abundance, wealth, health, and fertility, as well as joy and harmony in business, friendships, and family, for thousands of years. Whether it's an abundance of vitality and health, or calling in money and luck, green jade can stimulate a continuous flow of energy into our lives.

4. GREEN AVENTURINE
Considered the luckiest of all crystals, green aventurine is a stone of jubilant prosperity. On a deeper level, this stone harkens to the continuous renewal and boundless exaltation of nature, infusing our day with optimism, healing, and vitality and reminding us of all the ways in which we are already abundant.

5. PERIDOT
Peridot embodies the essence of early summer: sun-filled days, birdsong, and abundant green life bursting forth. Peridot's energy of prosperity, increase, and joy-filled ease inspires gratitude and generosity, refuting a scarcity mindset. Peridot reminds us that giving and receiving are both necessary halves of the same abundant whole. Tapping into wealth doesn't mean stealing it from someone else, as when we allow ourselves to be fully open to all the possibilities of life, there is enough for every one of us.

6. GOLDEN TOPAZ
When our will aligns with that of the Universe, there is nothing we cannot manifest for ourselves. Golden topaz, also known as imperial topaz, helps us discern which goals and desires are actually for our highest good. Once we have found that clarity, golden topaz shows us how to utilize a combination of focused intention and purposeful action to manifest the prosperous life of our dreams.

7. MOSS AGATE
While many desire immediate abundance, moss agate reminds us that in nature the most lasting growth is usually incremental. A stone of balance and stability, moss agate encourages planting seeds for the future over instant gratification of harvesting today, and is an excellent crystal for new investments or businesses hoping to grow over time.

CRYSTALS FOR SAFETY & PROTECTION

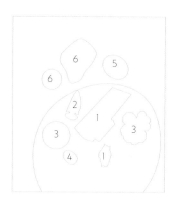

A need for safety is the most basic, universal, and primal of instincts. Without safety there is no foundation on which to dream, to desire, and to create. Feeling safe, secure, and protected means we can shift from simply surviving to making conscious choices in order to thrive.

I feel safe releasing my fears. It is safe to be here, and it is safe to be me.

1. BLACK TOURMALINE

The ultimate stone of protection, black tourmaline wards against and neutralizes destructive or unsafe energies, whether mental, emotional, spiritual, or physical. Use black tourmaline to grid the corners of your home, keep it on your desk, or wear it throughout the day to shield you in challenging situations.

2. BLACK OBSIDIAN

Formed of volcanic glass, black obsidian has been used for 700,000 years, as tools, weaponry, mirrors, and shamanic ritual items, by virtually every culture with access to it. Psychically and energetically protective, this sharp stone removes harmful energetic cords, attachments, and hooks, banishes dark energy from spaces, and illuminates the sources of obstruction within ourselves. Black obsidian is not a gentle stone, so be sure you're ready to have the truth reflected back to you. Use gold or sheen obsidian for a less intense energy.

3. SMOKY QUARTZ

Smoky quartz is a gentler protective stone, and one I recommend for empaths and children. Unlike black tourmaline, which blocks, or black obsidian that shreds or sends back harmful frequencies, smoky quartz creates an energetic shield that filters and grounds unaligned energies back to the Earth to be transmuted. Put in a pocket or wear for soft safeguarding, keep by the bed to absorb nightmares, or use in the house to create a space of safety.

4. JET

Jet, like many of its carbon-based cousins, is a natural energetic purifier, and has been popular since Roman times up to the Victorian era as an amulet for protection against ill intentions, physical danger, and malevolent spirits. Grounding, steadying, and practical, jet helps us differentiate between what might actually be harmful and what are merely shadows upon the wall. Jet is also a potent neutralizer and draws out the poison of denser vibrations within objects, spaces, or within ourselves, grounding and clearing the energy until once again aligned.

5. STICHTITE

This purple stone is spiritually protective as it helps us connect with our ever-present angels, guides, and guardians who are always there for us to call upon. Emotionally, stichtite prevents us from being gaslit, or pulled into another's drama or denser energetic field. Stichtite advises us to keep our hearts and minds open, but that healthy compassion is only possible through loving detachment. Above all, stichtite reminds us that no matter what happens, we are resilient beings who are divinely protected.

6. MALACHITE

One of the very few masculine-energied Heart chakra stones, malachite wards by restabilizing the heart's energetic field. It's common knowledge that the heart's electrical field is about 60 times greater in amplitude than that of the brain, and malachite, made from amplifying copper, is a ward that heals, strengthens, and thus expands this massive frequency even more, creating an energetic shield around us. Malachite shows us how to advocate for our own safety, to change or leave the situation that is harming us, and to take the necessary steps so we can actually live in a heart-centered way.

CRYSTALS FOR EASING STRESS & SOOTHING ANXIETY

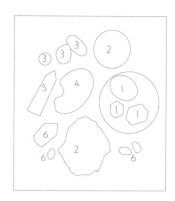

Stress and anxiety have become ubiquitious, so regulating our nervous system is paramount to our well-being. These crystals can supplement meditation, dancing, deep breathing, or even hugging to shift ourselves from a sympathetic (fight or flight) to a parasympathetic (rest and integrate) state.

I release anxiety and embrace the peace within me.

1. AMETHYST

A crystal of protection, purification, and tranquility, amethyst has been associated with lessening the hold harmful habits have on us since the time of the ancient Greeks. We all develop habits to regulate ourselves and to feel safe, but those often end up becoming unsupportive or even destructive later in life. Amethyst asks us to release what no longer serves us, and instead trust. Amethyst soothes while helping us move through the discomfort of change, growth, and expansion with more grace and ease.

2. LEPIDOLITE

This purple to pink mica is one of the most supportive stones when we're experiencing times of stress or depression. Containing natural lithium, lepidolite balances our mental and emotional states, soothes insomnia and nightmares, and alleviates anxiety and worry. Lepidolite is especially aligned with the vagus nerve, helping us shift from heightened alertness to peaceful awareness.

3. BLUE LACE AGATE

A calming and centering Throat chakra stone, blue lace agate encourages us not to be silenced by the anxieties we carry. This variety of agate radiates a peaceful energy, smoothing out extreme emotional spikes and helping us recognize what's causing the stress within our lives. Bolstering our ability to communicate our needs effectively and healthily, blue lace agate asks us to breathe deeply and use our voice in order to create a more peaceful reality for ourselves.

4. CELESTITE

Softly infusing physical spaces with serenity, celestite purifies and calms by gently raising the frequency of our vibrational field. Often associated with angelic communication, celestite reminds us that however overwhelmed we might be feeling, we aren't alone, and shows us how to connect with our divine guidance for support. This is also a wonderful stone for children, as its sweet and reassuring energy can also support restful sleep and pleasant dreams.

5. HOWLITE

When our thoughts won't stop racing, howlite steps in to quieten an overactive mind. Patient and soothing, howlite helps us recognize when our emotional responses are appropriate, or just reactive, and supports an expanded perspective on the situation in which we find ourselves. Howlite encourages us to refocus on the truth of the present moment and to release the anxious thought patterns that keep us up at night, and then distract us from fully living during the day.

6. LITHIUM QUARTZ

Lithium-included quartz is a crystal of spiritual centeredness. By helping us tune into our Higher Self and transfer our awareness from what's outside of us to what is within, lithium quartz supports the release of negative attachments, stress, and fear, and ushers in space for peace and harmony both for ourselves and within our relationships.

CRYSTALS FOR MENTAL FOCUS & MEMORY

In an age when we can easily access information online, we need to remember how to think, discern, focus, and retain what is important. These stones resonates with the Third Eye, so call on them when you need clarity of perception, support in focusing, and enhancement of memory.

I direct where my thoughts and attention go.

1. FLUORITE

Fluorite, in any hue, is first and foremost a stone of mental clarity. The blue, purple, and clear varieties are especially supportive for reconnecting to our intuition and innate awareness. On a less spiritual plane, fluorite is also a potent stone for balancing the Third Eye chakra, clearing out those brain cobwebs, improving our ability to absorb and remember data, analyze patterns, and make decisions. Meditating with fluorite shows us how to organize our thoughts into a cohesive framework from which anything is possible.

2. BLUE CALCITE

Some of the most compelling insights arrive when we allow ourselves to daydream, when we allow our minds to slip from thought to thought, and give ourselves the freedom to see where we might end up. Blue calcite is a bit dreamy, gently supporting comprehension and encouraging the balance of a relaxed and open mind without losing the focus necessary to interpret the knowledge that comes our way. An ally for students, blue calcite keeps us calm during crunch time and helps us retain information quickly and without stress.

3. DUMORTIERITE

Dumortierite's energy is like a strong wind, sweeping away mental fog, confusion, and brain lethargy. A fibrous blue mineral that is typically found within pegmatites, quartz, or in blue aventurine (pictured here), dumortierite's skill lies in its ability to intellectually stimulate as well as heighten our spiritual perceptions. An advocate of the organized mind, dumortierite is supportive in both the act of learning and calling upon that knowledge through our memories. Through its qualities of both intelligence and wisdom, dumortierite reminds us that cerebral knowledge is important, but must always be tempered by our inner guidance.

4. LAZULITE

Working at the conscious, unconscious, and subconscious levels of the mind, lazulite seeks to bring awareness and understanding to the ways in which we think. This deep blue pyramidal crystal is a powerful ally for reprogramming subconscious beliefs and creating new neural pathways, yet just as adept at enhancing brain function, memory, and our ability to focus. Lazulite, a catalyst for revelations and transcendent awareness, shows us that all parts of the mind, working in harmony, are necessary to live a life of meaning and purpose.

5. BLUE SAPPHIRE

In Vedic Astrology, blue sapphire is associated with the planet Saturn, but its correlation with knowledge, concentration, mental discipline, and discernment can also be found in many cultures beyond India. When we need help focusing on intellectual tasks, blue sapphire steps in to clear away distractions. A vigorous gemstone of the mind, blue sapphire reminds us to look beyond the obvious, think things through, and ask questions to find the truth of a matter before making decisions. This blue variety of corundum is also a protective ally for countering adverse influences, mental manipulation, and unhealthy thought patterns.

6. SODALITE

When we're buzzing with ideas or concepts but can't seem to grab hold, sodalite slows down our stream of consciousness just enough for us to comprehend those brilliant flashes of insight. Steadier and more grounded than most Third Eye or Throat chakra crystals, sodalite deepens our ability to think and process seemingly disparate information into a comprehensive whole that can be methodically communicated. Sodalite supports us in expressing our thoughts, helping us to disseminate our acumen, notions, and knowledge into the world.

CRYSTALS FOR COMMUNICATION

When we talk, write, sign, or use body language, we communicate with others. When we pray or chant, we speak to something larger than ourselves. These Throat chakra stones will help us express ourselves with authenticity, while still remaining open to really hearing those around us.

When I express myself clearly and honestly, I am heard.

1. AMAZONITE
It takes courage to be honest and strip away the conditioning of others and realize what is actually true for us. It takes even more courage to offer up our truth to another. Amazonite, a stone of courageous, authentic communication, asks us to do just that. It supports compassionate conversations and helps us connect and be heard, while reminding us to hear the truth of others.

2. AQUAMARINE
Aquamarine helps our words flow with ease. When tempers flare or we suppress feelings, aquamarine cools and soothes, supporting emotional release and self-regulation through clear communication. It dissolves energetic blockages in the Throat chakra, allowing words we may have been swallowing to rise and flow out with the tide. It shows that communication can be as healing and life-giving as water.

3. CHRYSOCOLLA
Gentle chrysocolla supports the channeling of our emotions and speaking from the heart. Aligned with Divine Feminine energy, it shows us how to release our creativity and articulate the rich depth of our emotional life without infringing on others. There is huge strength in speaking from a place of emotional vulnerability, and chrysocolla encourages us to do just that. It is supportive for musicians, writers, teachers, or public speakers who might benefit from connecting to their emotional truth first in order to communicate well with those around them.

4. LAPIS LAZULI
An ancient stone of pharaohs and goddesses, lapis lazuli typifies and embodies all the wisdom of the night sky. A Third Eye and Throat chakra stone, it stimulates mental and psychic abilities, and is aligned with the transmission of wisdom and truth. Ideal for performers, influencers, or leaders, lapis helps us understand the full impact we can have when we communicate. It also cautions that this should always be tempered with discernment: we must be aware of the responsibility this impact can have and be sure our words aren't weaponized to hurt or harm, but rather used to inspire, teach, and heal.

5. SHATTUCKITE
One of the best stones for spiritual connection, whether with our guides, ancestors, or guardian angels, shattuckite helps us connect to, receive, and fully understand their messages. It also supports the awakening of our natural-born claires (see page 140) and is helpful for channeling and interpreting the Tarot, runes, and other divination tools. Above all, shattuckite asks us to trust our inner truth, trust our guides and their messages, and most importantly, trust ourselves to speak.

6. TURQUOISE
The myths of turquoise date back millennia and span the globe. A talisman for protection and courage when traveling or in battle, turquoise was thought to be pieces of fallen sky and so was used in rituals to bring rain. Similarly, it can help us ask for what we need. Today, turquoise is used to facilitate communication, whether with the Universe, the inner self, or others.

7. BLUE ARAGONITE
Blue aragonite lets us hear our inner heart and speak to our spiritual self. It links the Crown to the Heart chakra, rebalancing the upper energy centers through the expression of the Throat. This stone is perfect for spiritual communication via chanting, meditation, or soundwork, and also supportive of philosophical dialogue, easing the relay of spiritual concepts. Associated with water, the element of emotions, it helps us express feelings in a way that is harmonizing.

CRYSTALS FOR MAGIC & INTUITION

Intuition is our ability to perceive the subtle frequencies around us, and magic is our ability to align ourselves to influence them. They're both energetic versions of what we already do physically. We're divine beings capable of influencing, manifesting, and co-creating reality—and that is truly magical.

I trust my intuition, and am attuned to the wisdom and magic of the Universe.

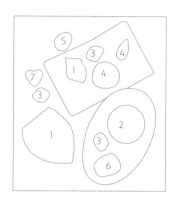

1. AMETHYST
Believed to activate the pineal gland, the seat of the Third Eye chakra, amethyst promotes an awareness of the world's subtle energetics. It soothes reactive emotions and tumultuous thoughts, and helps us release unhelpful beliefs and habits. In doing this, we can focus on the present and what our intuition is telling us in order to take aligned action. Amethyst protects our energetic field, bolstering our connection with the divine and our intuitive abilities.

2. INDIGO GABBRO (mystic merlinite)
Indigo gabbro correlates with both the Third Eye and Root chakras, activating our mind, anchoring our body, and clearing blockages in our field to support the realization of our dormant psychic gifts. This crystal asks us to look within to see where we might be holding ourselves back, what karma needs to be released, or pieces of ourselves retrieved in order to reclaim our magical talents.

3. MOONSTONE
Like moonlight incarnate, moonstone teaches us how to notice the glimmers of intuition when they come to us. It asks us to release analytical thinking, close our physical eyes, and allow ourselves to truly see. By embracing the wisdom found in the dark hours of the night, and recognizing the illuminating insights within ourselves, moonstone helps us witness the magic of life and accept our mystical place within it.

4. LABRADORITE
Anyone seeing labradorite immediately understands why it's associated with magic as this dark stone flashes with brilliant colors in direct light. These hidden yet dazzling rainbows reflect the magic within everything, including ourselves. Labradorite brings our spiritual gifts into the light of day and heightens our awareness of the energetics within physical objects, making this ideal for healers or body workers. A quintessential companion or tool for magical rituals or any divinatory practice, labradorite reminds us of the magic of which we're capable.

5. IOLITE
Iolite speaks to us of visions and voyages. A stone of spiritual and shamanic journeys, it acts as an inner compass and enhances the clarity of visions during meditation, past-life regression, or astral projection. It stimulates our Third Eye chakra, strengthens intuition, and aids access to the spiritual realms and the knowledge therein.

6. BLUE JADE
Blue jadeite clears the mind of intrusive thoughts and creates space for us to hear our spiritual guides and Highest Self. This rare stone is like a teacher during times of psychic discovery, helping us navigate these periods with more grace and ease. A crystal of spiritual knowledge, blue jade asks us to keep our minds open, and reminds us that intuitive insight can come from anywhere: meditation, altered states of consciousness, dreams, philosophical debates, and even mundane conversations.

7. MERLINITE
Not to be confused with mystic merlinite, this stone is associated with the magic of duality. We cannot have light without dark: they are ever entwined. Merlinite rejects spiritual bypassing and the ego-based desire to be special and instead invites us to look deeper. An alchemist transforms herself while endeavoring to turn lead into gold, while a mystic spends decades delving into his soul to glean the wisdom of subtle energy. Merlinite enjoins us to turn inward—to explore, integrate, and transmute our own shadow-self. In doing so, we gain an understanding of how magic works, and become adept at calibrating ourselves in order to influence the suble energy around us.

CRYSTALS FOR SLEEPING & DREAMING

We sleep for a third of our lives, yet the importance of this nightly sojourn is often overlooked. Missing even a few hours of sleep affects the body's ability to function and a lack of dreams can slowly starve the soul. It is fascinating that we're at our most vulnerable while asleep, but also our most powerful: able to travel through time and space, rewrite our histories, and even meet guides or ancestors. Here, the first selection focuses on stones to support relaxing into a deep and regenerative sleep, while the second highlights crystals particularly potent for all types of dreamwork. To utilize these stones, speak your intention out loud, then keep them by the bed, under your pillow, or even create a crystal grid on your nightstand.

I fall asleep effortlessly, and am safe when I dream.

SLEEP

1. LEPIDOLITE
Lepidolite's natural inclination to calm and soothe makes it an ideal companion during slumber. Emotional upheavals and runaway thoughts can cause insomnia, or once asleep and we are at our most vulnerable, nightmares. Lepidolite gently absorbs the anxiety and stress of the day that might stay with us into our evenings and soothes the nervous system to ease us into restful and restorative sleep.

2. CELESTITE
Named for its celestial connections, celestite asks us to trust that our guardian angels are always looking out for our best interests, and to sleep deeply, knowing they are watching over us. Even if one doesn't believe in angels, celestite's natural ethereal energy brings an aura of peace, tranquility, and safety into any space in which it's placed, purifying lower vibrations while helping us unwind the tension of reactivity and hypervigilance, then soften into gentle slumber. This is also a wonderful crystal for those prone to nightmares, as its sweet, reassuring energy supports pleasant dreams.

3. BLUE SCHEELITE (lapis lace onyx)
Formed of alternating bands of luminous blue calcite and dolomite, blue scheelite isn't a scheelite at all, and the name is actually a misnomer. But the mistaken name doesn't diminish its energy of peaceful, calming stability. Blue scheelite is a synergistic combination,

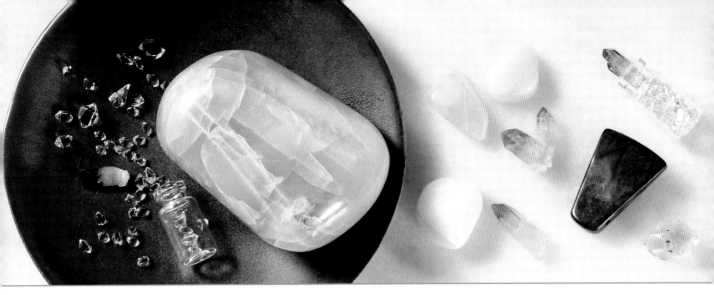

helping us return from the spirals of worry or spiked emotions back to the present moment with a sense of spaciousness and serenity, which is especially helpful during the dark hours of the night. While the blue calcite quietens our thoughts, the dolomite softens our emotions, the two working together harmoniously to deepen our connection to the balanced inner self and drift straight to sleep.

4. AMETHYST

Ever versatile, amethyst is a perfect and readily available crystal to keep in a healing space to encourage relaxation, or by the bedside when you need help dropping off into dreamland. A crystal of purification, amethyst acts as a filter, cleansing the room—and by extension our own auric field—of disharmonious energies. Amethyst is also supportive of releasing the unaligned habits that contribute to unhealthy sleep patterns. A peaceful protector of the mind and spirit, amethyst steps up while we sleep, shielding us from unnecessary nightmares and helping us become more aware of why we might be having them in the first place.

DREAMS

1. HERKIMER DIAMOND

A rare quartz that naturally forms into a diamond shape as it grows, a Herkimer diamond may be small, but it is also an energetic powerhouse. Extremely high-frequencied, Herkimer diamond not only emanates its own energy of pure light, but also purifies, holds, and amplifies our intentions out into the ether of the world, creating ripples of change in the physical realm. Herkimer diamond is equally potent when we are asleep as when we're awake, and is one of the best crystals to work with for engaging in astral travel or timeline-jumping, to clarify our inner vision, connect to other dimensions, and as an enhancement for all forms of meditation and dreamwork.

2. VERA CRUZ AMETHYST

One of the highest vibrational forms of amethyst, Vera Cruz amethyst is a crystal of pure spiritual light. An ally on our ascension spiral, Vera Cruz brings awareness of where we are in the present moment and, by balancing the hemispheres of the brain, invokes harmony between the mind and spirit. While we sleep, Vera Cruz supports intentional dream-journeying and safeguards us during our unconscious wanderings. Vera Cruz shows us how to stay present and aware of our dream state while lucid dreaming, and encourages us to recognize the power we have to effect change during this potent time.

3. MOONSTONE

Moonstone, in any color, has been associated with the night-clad time of dreaming, mystery, and insight for thousands of years. Shimmering moonstone asks us to seek the light in the dark and the wisdom within our own souls; to let ourselves be led by our own intuition, for it will never fail us. A stone associated with the Goddess, moonstone offers her tender assurances that we are safe to dream, keeping at bay nightmares unless we truly need them to process our fears, and opening the way for us to dream what we most need in order to heal, expand, and become wise. Moonstone then helps us remember and understand our dreams upon waking, so we can continue to hold on to the insights gleaned during the night.

4. SUGILITE

Sugilite enhances the depth and vividness of daydreams, night journeys, and meditative visions. Activating the Third Eye and Crown chakras, sugilite incites lucid dreaming, invites us to perceive the infinite possibilities available to us when we are asleep, and then maintain that expansive perspective into our waking world. Sugilite summons our soul's deeply buried dreams and desires to the surface, helping us recognize and remember our purpose via the symbols and stories playing through our unconscious each night. Light-infusing and protective, sugilite wards our mind and energetic body by raising our own frequency to match its own, dissolving harmful attachments and shielding us from night terrors.

CRYSTALS FOR CREATIVITY & ARTISTIC EXPRESSION

Art has many benefits, not least letting us express our feelings and connect to something greater than ourselves. Conditioning, criticism, and rejection can make it difficult for us to sing, paint, write, craft, or build, but these stones support our endeavors, however we are called to express ourselves.

I allow myself to be open to my creative flow, and express myself without fear.

1. CARNELIAN
Often turned to in order to inflame physical passion or encourage fertility, carnelian is just as much a stone of artistic and entrepreneurial creation. Passions, whether of the body or of the soul, are both housed within the Sacral chakra, and this red-banded agate is the ultimate stone for both. Carnelian shows us how to seize the present moment, take pleasure in what inspires us, and to give in to the call of what the muses wish to be born through us.

2. CHRYSOCOLLA
Chrysocolla is a crystal of communication, but it's also a stone of the heart, asking us to burrow deep into our joy, and love, and sorrow, and pain, and instead of losing ourselves, channel those emotions and experiences to create. For art that stirs the soul isn't formed by intellectual exercise or algorithms. Art that moves us is a wave formed deep within one person's heart and poured forth into another's through music, dance, paint, or poetry. Chrysocolla shows us how, through art, we become more human, while through creative expression, we become more whole.

3. VANADINITE
Starting and finishing: two of the most challenging parts of creating. The blank page and the long haul are frightening in equal measure, and that is where vanadanite wishes to support us. This vibrant red stone is a muse and coach in one, opening the space for inspiration, encouraging us to begin when we are struck with the creative urge, and then energizing us to see it through to completion. Vanadanite lends us the stamina needed to bring our novel, course, new business, or work of art fully formed into the world.

4. TANGERINE QUARTZ
This joy-filled, orange-stained quartz is one of curiosity, exploration, and the exuberance that comes from making something new. While in adults it can also stimulate sexual passion, tangerine quartz still holds a frequency of innocence and playfulness. Those long summer days, imagining worlds through which we ran as children, still reside within us. Tangerine quartz encourages us never to stop playing, and never to stop dreaming up stories and games, for that is where true inspiration lies.

5. SODALITE
Sodalite, the "Writer's Stone," supports the translation of our thoughts, ideas, and creative genius into the right words for expression. It enhances our observational insight, inviting us to be inspired by the sheer variety of wit and wisdom to be found in our world. Sodalite deepens our ability to think and then graciously helps us transform those thoughts into words to continue impacting the world around us.

6. WULFENITE (not pictured)
An alchemic stone of catalyzation, wulfenite asks, "what if?" What if we weren't afraid? What if it didn't matter what others think? What if we believed we're worthy of our art and that it is good enough just because it exists? What if meaning also comes from what we channel into it? What if we let ourselves be seized by the magic of inspiration and allow the beauty of creation to pour forth? Wulfenite, activating the Solar Plexus and Sacral chakras, shows us how to overcome creative blocks and a fear of failure, encourages us to leap into the artistic unknown, and continues to cheer for us until our endeavor is fully manifested.

CRYSTALS FOR VITALITY & HEALTH

Humans have turned to crystals for their perceived restorative properties for millennia. While stones shouldn't replace modern medicine, you can use energetically aligned stones to facilitate healing. The crystals below are perfect to stimulate general healing, vitality, and physical wellness.

When I lovingly care for my body and honor its needs, it has space to heal and thrive.

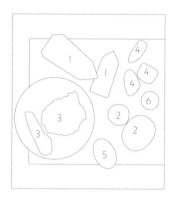

1. GOLDEN HEALER QUARTZ

Golden healer quartz is believed to be one of the best stones for any type of physical healing. Activating light codes within us, golden healer asks us to remember we are divine beings, and within each one of us lies the power to heal ourselves, completely and fully, if that is what is most aligned for our journey in this life. This Solar Plexus and Crown chakra stone shows us how to be our own healers and advocates, and helps us shift the beliefs and behaviors that are stopping us from embodying the vitality that's possible. A catalyst, golden healer empowers us to take action for our own well-being, inviting us to trust what our bodies are telling us and what our intuition says we most need.

2. HEMATOID QUARTZ

This beautiful, red-swirled quartz is one to reach for when in need of physical, emotional, or mental balance and stability. The hematite inclusions support our ability to ground, especially when we are feeling dissociated, scattered, confused, or lethargic, while the quartz amplifies and helps us tap into the steady natural life force to which we always have access. Hematoid quartz helps us tune into the natural rhythms of our own bodies, so we can flourish physically.

3. RED CALCITE

Calcites naturally have a gentler energy than other stones, and red calcite is no different, inviting a steady stream of *prana* into our physical vessel without the intensity. Red calcite helps us appreciate our experience as physical beings, reminding us that our health and embodiment are meant to be enjoyed and explored, not just utilized for productivity. Red calcite is also supportive during the process of detoxification, showing us how the establishment of healthy habits and boundaries can raise our energetic vibration as well as promote our physical well-being.

4. RED JASPER

Red jasper is a stone of stability, stamina, and physical strength. Instead of grounding our energy back to the ley lines of the Earth, this variety of jasper helps us connect to and invite an infusion of Gaia's vitality into the body via the Root chakra. When we're feeling tired or run-down, red jasper shows us how to nourish ourselves for the long haul. Restorative red jasper purifies the energy that's become sluggish within our auric field and chakra system, helping the flow of our inner life force to circulate with more ease and vigor.

5. UNAKITE JASPER

While the other crystals here focus on energetic or physical healing, unakite understands that our physical challenges are often rooted in emotional suffering that has been subsumed by the body. Unakite, patient and sure, encourages us to feel into our pain and examine our injuries. What was happening at that time? What anger or anguish were we not allowed to express when young? What harmful habits have we developed to cope? Unakite shows us how to release repressed emotions and patterns of pain over time, healing both our hearts and bodies.

6. MOOKAITE (mook jasper)

Mookaite is an energetically slow but deeply moving jasper found only in Western Australia. Nurturing and wise, mookaite asks us to slow down too, to notice the world around us and the world within. It reminds us that time isn't meant to be hurried through. It ebbs and flows, and by sinking deep into slow and steady awareness, we can even repair our own cells, potentially slowing the physical aging process. Connecting to the eternal, boundless timelines of the Earth, mookaite helps us heal our ancestral lineages and the genes within ourselves that have been damaged by intergenerational trauma, restoring the vitality that was ours all along.

CRYSTALS FOR CONNECTING TO SELF

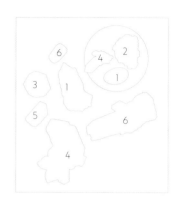

Each and every one of us is a unique, divine being, but from birth society tries to homogenize and condition us. As we grow, it can be harder to hear our own heart, but with awareness can break the cycle, supported by these powerful stones to journey back to ourselves.

I honor the whispers of my body, heart, and soul, and allow them to guide me.

1. ASTROPHYLLITE

When we are feeling lost, confused, or apathetic about our place in life, astrophyllite, with its starburst of copper and gold, points the way. A catalyzing stone of transformation, astrophyllite reminds us why we chose this particular life, and asks us to remember our true purpose and reason for being born. It asks: What lights us up? What brings us peace? Helping us let go of conditioning and reorienting to the magnetic north of our inner sense of knowing, astrophyllite supports our recognition of the path that is in the highest alignment for us.

2. NIRVANA QUARTZ

Found high in the Himalayas, nirvana quartz, or "ice quartz," formed as it was carved by expanding and retreating glaciers over millennia. This is a crystal that has experienced what it's like to be hurt, to be worn away, to be scarred by life in a cycle that doesn't seem to end, and yet, that is precisely how it gained its wisdom. Nirvana quartz demonstrates that to reach enlightenment, we must first fully accept our experiences as part of our journey toward wisdom, and then fully accept and have compassion for ourselves, scars and all, to break the cycle and reach Nirvana. Nirvana quartz asks us to trust the process of self-catalyzation.

3. ALMANDINE GARNET

Resonating with the lower chakras, garnet asks us to remember we are physical, embodied beings living in a physical world. Whether we are disconnected from our bodies due to pain or illness, or we reject our physical selves due to guilt and shame, garnet reminds us that all those sensations are just the body's way of communicating, and there is wisdom to be found if we will only listen. Garnet helps us to see that our physical vessel was never meant to be our enemy, and can be very supportive, both for embracing our sensual desires and to reconnect and find compassion for ourselves during times of injury or illness.

4. CHLORITE PHANTOM QUARTZ

So called because of the green layers outlining a ghostly crystal within the quartz, chlorite phantom enables us to see the phases of its own growth. Just as we can peek into the crystal's history, chlorite phantom quartz asks us to look inside ourselves and remember who we used to be, the phases we've gone through, and how we've grown, and changed, and healed. Chlorite itself is a mineral of regeneration, and combined with the amplification of quartz, is supportive for the continuation of both physical and emotional healing. Chlorite phantom reminds us that when we can fully understand our journey thus far, where we currently stand and what is next for us become much clearer.

5. DRAVITE (brown tourmaline)

When we shut parts of ourselves away, we can never be whole. When we begin to open the door to face our shadows, our triggers and traumas can at times feel overwhelming, but dravite is here to help us move through the integration process with tenderness and hope. Keeping us steady through its grounding influence, brown tourmaline helps us see what parts of ourselves still need to heal, still need to be brought into the light and shown love, and then helps us do just that.

6. BLUE KYANITE

A crystal of bridges and connections, blue kyanite shows us how to connect to others, our spiritual guides, and, just as potently, to ourselves. Often utilized for opening the Third Eye, meditation, and spiritual communication, blue kyanite supports a reconnection with our Higher Self, as well as aiding the disparate parts of our physical, emotional, mental, and energetic bodies to come together once again into a state of aligned integrity.

CRYSTALS FOR CONNECTING TO EARTH

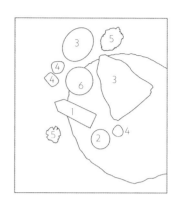

Our natural tether to Earth is deep and intuitive, but it has become harder to hear the song of the leaves, to commune with animals, to feel connected to a greater whole, and both we and the Earth are suffering for it. The crystals below are especially aligned for reconnecting to the natural world.

I am grateful for my deep and strong roots that allow the energy of the earth to flow through me.

1. MOSS AGATE/TREE AGATE

These sister stones connect us to the growing life of the world and the nature spirits within. They tune us into the abundance of the natural world, while also showing us how to treat it with respect. We aren't meant to take, but to exist in a state of constant energetic exchange with our tree, grass, fern, and flower siblings. Moss and tree agates, similar to their namesakes, are both energetically slower moving, providing us with a calm, balanced stability during periods of growth, and are also supportive during times of slow-and-steady physical recovery.

2. SHAMAN STONE

Resonating with both the Root and Earth Star chakras, shaman stone is an energizing yet grounding stone, helping us anchor into our bodies and back to the land. Formed of earth and iron, shaman stone holds the frequency of the Earth and naturally takes two shapes: a round Feminine and an acorn/discus Masculine. Holding one of each is thought to realign the magnetic polarity within the body, reorienting us back to the Schumann Frequency. Working with a pair of shaman stones can be powerful, but even one can support shamanic journeying, soul retrieval, dreamwork, animal communication, and reconnecting with the soul of our planet.

3. PETRIFIED WOOD

Made from ancient trees transformed into silicate, opal, or stone, petrified wood is a physical manifestation of the timelessness of our planet. Always changing, always evolving, yet eternal. When we're harried, triggered, disoriented, or even frightened, petrified wood resonates with the steady frequency of patience, stability, and inner peace, allowing us to tap into its ancient perspective. It asks us to trust our Earth Mother and not to fight our transformation and steady growth, reminding us to stay in our bodies while we let our energetic roots burrow into the earth when we need support.

4. SERAPHINITE

A green clinochlore, seraphinite embodies the resonance of Gaia Sophia—the very heart and soul of our planet. The ancient belief that the Earth is a mother goddess who gave birth to us all stretches across the globe. Seraphinite asks us to remember that bond, to feel the vibration of Gaia's eternal words beneath our feet and in our bones, which will one day return to her. It lets us see flashes of the divine within the earthy mundane, showing us they are one and the same. Seraphinite is a stone of spiritual, emotional, and physical self-healing and regeneration, just as Gaia regenerates one way or another.

5. STAR ARAGONITE

Star aragonite is one of the few Earth Star stones, renewing and balancing the energetic center beneath our feet, as well as the Root. Able to draw higher light frequencies down the chakra column to be integrated into our physical body, star aragonite also draws energy up, strengthening our energetic tether to the Earth's ley lines. Its purpose is twofold: by anchoring our connection to Gaia it enwraps us in a steadying yet energizing web of light, but we also transfer the energy Gaia needs to heal via the same tether. Star aragonite highlights the interdependence between all living things and the Earth, and encourages us to take responsibility for ourselves and our world.

6. SERPENTINE

Serpents have been associated with Earth Wisdom and Earth Magic since ancient times as their bodies are connected to the land, and their cycle of shedding is reminiscent of the Earth's renewal through the seasons. Serpentine is imbued with this energy, helping us reconnect to the natural world, tap into the Akashic Records, and access the wisdom and healing on offer from Gaia herself. Please note that serpentine can also begin the Kundalini Awakening process, so be very clear in your intentions with this stone.

CRYSTALS FOR SPIRITUAL AWAKENING

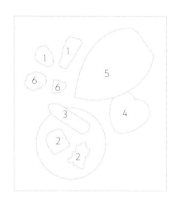

Many in the spiritual community believe we are in a transitional period for the collective, a time of mass awakening. These stones focus on the spiritual growth possible for each of us, supporting our meditation practice, self-awareness, inner transformation, and connection to Higher Self.

I surrender to the call within my soul to awaken.

1. CAVANSITE

Cavansite is a crystal of consciousness expansion and spiritual revelation. When we seek to wade into the waters of soul awakening, it encourages us to jump in and dive deep, immersing ourselves in the wonders ready to unfold around us. Cavansite shows us that living with curiosity and intention creates opportunities for spiritual breakthroughs with every interaction. Via meditation or shamanic journeying, cavansite helps us to unlock our psychic abilities and access the Akashic Records, the fabled records of all existence and knowledge within the Universe.

2. CLEAR APOPHYLLITE

The clear/white variety of apophyllite is a gentle but potent higher vibrational crystal adept at raising the frequency of our space and our own energetic field. One of the best crystals to aid in meditation work, apophyllite supports us in establishing connections to higher dimensional beings and receiving wisdom from our Over Soul. A stone of sacred light, apophyllite helps us move through the feelings of disillusionment, apathy, or discouragement that can arise on our spiritual journey, and experience again the elation and peace that enfolds us when we are living in alignment with our Highest Self.

3. DANBURITE

Danburite sings of the peace available when connected to Source. Associated with angelic communication and channeling, danburite is a powerful meditation tool, an ally when we wish to let go of the annoyances of daily life and focus instead on the divine joy found in small, miraculous moments. Danburite connects the Heart, Crown, and Soul Star chakras, showing us the inherent link between love of Self and the Divine Love of all. It is this realization that can help us truly begin to expand as souls.

4. PURPLE/LAVENDER JADE

Associated with the Buddhist goddess Kwan Yin, believed to have achieved enlightenment through her extraordinary compassion, this jade shows us how to follow the same path. When we increase our capacity to hold compassion for ourselves and those around us, we begin moving into a state of increased serenity. This may not feel easy, but developing a practice of compassion, without giving up our boundaries, is an intrinsic part of our spiritual journey. Knowing what is right for us, while holding compassion for what isn't, is a mark of an evolved soul. Purple jadeites can also deepen our meditation practice, helping us gain a wider perspective of the world and our place within it.

5. TROLLEITE

Trolleite, the "Stone of Awakening," is a powerful ally in our ascension journey, helping us to attune with our Higher Self and be better able to hear our guardian angels and ethereal mentors. Trolleite can act as a crystalline guide on our journey of self-awareness, even helping us understand the events of other lifetimes pushing us to evolve in this one. It heightens our meditation and alternative-state work, and grants us the calm collectiveness of self to explore the expansiveness of life, the Earth, and the Universe, so we can continue to evolve as souls.

6. MOLDAVITE

The most well-known tektite, moldavite is a meteoric glass of rapid spiritual evolution, so highly vibrational it positively buzzes and our own energy cannot help but seek to entrain its frequencies. This can lead to unexpected changes in relationships or work situations, or manifest as physical symptoms as our body tries to detox rapidly. Moldavite should be treated with respect intentionally. When we're ready, it can offer the chance to accelerate transformation and spiritual ascension, purging the chakras of unaligned attachments, increasing synchronicities, awakening awareness, and helping us see who we're truly meant to be.

CRYSTALS FOR NEW BEGINNINGS & LETTING GO

Beginnings and endings are two sides of the same coin. We cannot begin anew until we let the old fall away, and without a beginning there is no ending. This endless cycle of birth, death, and rebirth is reflected externally by the seasons and in the phases of the Moon, but we feel it most keenly in our day-to-day lives. We aren't meant to stagnate, but the transitions between having a job and losing it, breaking up and feeling safe enough to love again, releasing old conditioning, and even moving between an old and new home can feel overwhelming. These stones are divided into two sections, but each has wisdom to share for how to release what is no longer ours to hold on to and embrace the new possibilities that life is offering us.

I release what no longer is, and trust in this new beginning.

NEW BEGINNINGS

1. BLACK MOONSTONE

As the Moon waxes and wanes, its energy shifts and its pull on us shifts at the same time. Black moonstone taps into the magic of the New Moon, that dark void where anything becomes possible and the traditional time to envision, set intentions, and start endeavors. This dark variety of moonstone is a perfect ally for amplifying those dreams germinating within us, and a good support for beginning anew, reminding us that the unknown of transition is only temporary, and how natural change can be if we only allow it.

2. FLOWER AGATE

Flower agate is a newly discovered stone formed of beautiful plumes of chalcedony within the agate, forming sweet pink petal and flower formations. This crystal carries with it a joyfulness, encouraging us to plant those metaphorical seeds and delight in the process of watching them bloom. Flower agate is particularly supportive of burgeoning relationships, new projects or careers, and our own self-development.

3. AMMONITE

This curled fossilized sea creature encapsulates the movement inherent within the Sacred Spiral of life. Only living in the newest and largest chamber of its shell as it grows, ammonite reminds us to keep moving forward and not to be afraid to step into the new life we are creating for ourselves. In a more practical sense,

ammonites are also powerful supporters of the movement associated with buying, selling, or finding a new home, and can be a useful ally during this process.

4. CHRYSOPRASE

Chrysoprase speaks to us of new leaves unfurling from bare branches, new sprouts pushing forth into the sun, and the optimism of springtime. This compassionate green stone is one of regeneration, physical and emotional healing, open-hearted and joy-filled love, and the promise of growth into something new, something even more aligned and beautiful. Chrysoprase invites us to shake off the habits and protective measures of a long winter and marvel that we, like nature, always contain within ourselves the capacity to begin again in any and all areas of our lives.

LETTING GO

1. APACHE TEAR

Apache tear is so called due to the myth of it forming from the tears of the Apache women who wept over their fallen sons and husbands. As the myth suggests, this type of obsidian is the quintessential stone for grief and loss. Apache tear energetically holds us and keeps us safe while encouraging us to let go of the need to control what we feel, and instead, surrender to the torrent of emotions that comes after loss in a way that is supported. It gently reminds us that suppressing our grief and anger will only keep these discordant emotions stuck in our auric field, thus preventing or prolonging the healing process, and that tears are the way for our body to physically, emotionally, and energetically release the pain being held within. Apache tear shows us that mourning means we have loved, and that it is the first step in letting go.

2. DIOPTASE

Dioptase speaks to us of the transformational healing that can come when we are able to find compassion for those who have hurt us. A powerful crystal of emotional amelioration, dioptase shows us that in order to begin again, we must set down the weight of the woundings we have received, in this and in previous lifetimes. When we are reeling after a breakup or unable to form secure attachments because of abuse or childhood trauma, dioptase steps in to hold our hearts, whispering to us to let go, let go, let go of the anger that poisons us from the inside out, let go of the fear of being loved, and let go of the discordant energetic ties that were part of our path, but are no longer meant to be part of our journey.

3. GOLD SHEEN OBSIDIAN

Gold sheen obsidian is a potent stone of releasing what disempowers us. Gold sheen acts as a mirror, revealing the places in our lives where we are allowing others or situations to harm, diminish, or control us, and boldly asks us each to see ourselves as we truly are: not victims, but Divine Beings on a journey of expansion. This variety of obsidian shows us that the pain we are seeking to avoid is often still present because we are actually too afraid to let it go. We think holding tightly will keep us safer than facing the unknown. Gold sheen obsidian reveals the places of conditioning and supports us in transforming those triggers and fears into opportunities for stepping into a more expansive life.

4. RHODOCHROSITE

Rhodochrosite is a Heart chakra crystal of introspection. A loving pink stone, it asks us to look, really look, at our own hearts, witness, and have compassion for the self-judgment, self-hatred, shame, or guilt that we carry. Rhodochrosite helps us recognize what is actually ours, what was placed upon us that we believe to be ours, and the intergenerational trauma that shaped us in our mother's womb waters and lives within our very cells. It helps us understand the complexities of emotional healing and encourages us to forgive and release the attachments to the feelings and identities that aren't actually ours, creating space for us to rediscover who we were truly meant to be and the infinite possibilities before us.

CRYSTALS FOR CONNECTING TO ANGELS

Many cultures believe in divine intermediaries, messengers, guardians, or help-meets, if not the Abrahamic concept of angels. These crystals support connection with angelic entities, whether we wish to speak with angels during dreams or meditations, or manifest more everyday miracles.

I am always connected to the divine beings that protect and guide me.

1. AMPHIBOLE QUARTZ

Nicknamed "angel phantom quartz" due to the wispy, feathery amphibole inclusions within the quartz, amphibole quartz is a joy-filled crystal of spiritual awareness, inner growth, and angelic connection. Ranging from deep reds and yellows to silvers and blues, the phantoms in the quartz guide us inward—supporting a deeper understanding of ourselves through meditation—and then back out again, helping us witness the echoes of angels via chance encounters and "commonplace" miracles within our daily lives. Amphibole quartz asks us to look beyond the mundane and see how the divine moves within us all.

2. CELESTITE

Celestite, also known as celestine, is a gentle yet high-vibrational stone that's named for the soft blues of the heavens and its metaphysical ability to facilitate connection to celestial entities, angelic realms, and our guardian guides. Celestite is a peaceful stone, helping us find that calm space within and reassuring us we can always turn to our ethereal divine companions for guidance and protection. Celestite purifies physical spaces and helps us find the serenity necessary to access the celestial spheres through meditation and dreams.

3. SERAPHINITE

Patterned with chatoyant silvery green "feathers" of clinochlore and mica, seraphinite is named for the Seraphim, one of the highest orders of angels. Many angels have become associated with stars and celestial bodies; seraphinite is representative of the essence of Gaia Sophia, the angelic energetic embodiment of the soul of our planet. Linking the ethereal and the material, seraphinite is one of the few crystals that resonates with and reconnects us to both the angelic realms and the earthly, deepening our ability to commune with our angelic, animal, and plant guides. Nurturing seraphinite invites us to embrace the potential for healing and growth, whether spiritual, emotional, or physical.

4. ANGELITE (not pictured)

Angelite is a soothing stone of serene spirituality and compassionate communication. It helps us speak with our angels and guides, and through the act of expressing our inner truth to those beings who love us unconditionally, we allow the vulnerability necessary for those same angels and guides to help shift our pain into insight, clarity, and wholeness of self. Angelite supports in moments of fear or overwhelm, calming our nervous system and reminding us we are always protected.

5. ELESTIAL

While other stones in this collection facilitate communication with angels, elestial quartz draws the frequency of the higher realms down into our physical and etheric bodies, infusing high-vibrational light energy into our very cells. Through the grounding of our Higher Selves into our everyday lives, elestials support the ability for us to channel our own inner angel, enabling us to serve a divine purpose for others. Many believe elestials themselves are guardian crystal angels, energetically matched to a person for whom they will serve as a spiritual guide when the time is right.

6. DANBURITE

The sweet peace that emanates from danburite helps us release density and trapped emotions, clearing the mind and heart for pure divine radiance. A beautiful meditation tool and miracle-magnetizer, danburite facilitates communion with angels—not only receiving their messages more fully, but imbuing us with their divine light. White danburite supports the exploration of angelic realms through spiritual journeys, while pink danburite reminds us that we're worthy of the Divine Love always on offer, and capable of embodying and amplifying it out into the world for others.

DIVINE FEMININE & MASCULINE CRYSTALS

The Divine Feminine and Sacred Masculine were never meant to be at odds; one was never meant to dominate the other. Our world, our society, may feel increasingly polarized, but it's important to remember that we are all, whichever gender we resonate with or however we may identify, a synthesis of both these archetypal energies. Both are necessary for balance. The following collection can offer wisdom and support to find a way of honoring that equilibrium within ourselves and within the collective.

I can easily balance the Feminine & Masculine energies within myself, and draw upon their strengths when needed.

MORE CRYSTALS TO INVOKE THE DIVINE FEMININE
Chrysocolla (5), Lemurian quartz (6), Kunzite (7), Morganite (8), Rose quartz (9), Seraphinite (10), Aquamarine (11)

MORE CRYSTALS TO INVOKE THE SACRED MASCULINE
Golden Imperial Topaz (5), Red jasper (6), Malachite (7), Black tourmaline (8), Hematite (9), Black onyx (10), Bronzite (11)

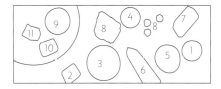

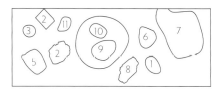

DIVINE FEMININE

1. LARIMAR
Found only in the Dominican Republic, this rare but highly sought-after stone is a beautiful embodiment of how power can be found in compassion and sensitivity. Like the water for which it's named, larimar is soothing to the emotional body and deeply connected to Goddess energy. Larimar shows us that the situation around us may ebb and flow with the tides, but that the water itself is always there. When we are self-aware, we are able to let go and flow with life. Larimar is also a crystal of clear communication and lovingly expressed boundaries, for our own pool must be full if it is to overflow for others.

2. PINK OPAL
Pink opal is a nurturer, holding our heart when it needs mending. One of the gentlest of crystals, pink opal dissipates the stress of trauma, eases loneliness and grief, is protective of sensitive souls and children, and supportive when our inner little one needs care. In the Andes, where the stone is found, pink opal was believed to have been a gift from Pachamama, the Incan goddess of the Earth, love, and fruitfulness. This calming and reassuring Divine Feminine crystal shows how joy and sorrow are both valid, and how to embrace the emotions of the moment without losing ourselves to them.

3. CUPRITE

A crystal of the earthen goddesses, red cuprite stimulates the Root and Sacral chakras, infusing our bodies with vitality. While many red stones are masculine-energied, outwardly focused on action, cuprite finds its power in its receptive abilities, helping us satisfy and meet our physical needs and aiding in the recuperation of wounds and illnesses. Cuprite is a crystal of Kundalini Awakening, physical and energetic fertility, and the swollen-bellied goddess, powerful in her internal creations soon to be birthed into the world.

4. MOONSTONE

Moonstone is one of the original and most well-known of the archetypal Divine Feminine gemstones. Acutely attuned to the lunar energy of the Goddess, moonstone invites us to tune into our intuition and initiates us into the mysteries of magic. Reflectively shimmering like its namesake, moonstone is a beacon of light when all seems dark, and a guide and protector when traveling, whether that be in the waking or dreaming world. Moonstone asks us to call upon her when we wish to embrace the Divine Feminine within each of us.

DIVINE MASCULINE

1. TIGER'S EYE

Tiger's eye is a stone of confidence, willpower, practicality, and enlightened action, supporting physical vitality and strength of the body and mind. Tiger's eye invites us to remember that the Sacred Masculine isn't an energy of reactionary, ego-based outbursts, but instead is calm, practical, discerning, and decisive, only taking action once all the scales have been weighed and the most balanced way forward presents itself. Tiger's eye supports mental and emotional equilibrium and also helps to release the patterns of toxic masculinity within all genders and gender identities.

2. PYRITE

A crystal of manifestation and wealth through purposeful action, pyrite encourages us to be the "fire starters" and catalyzers for ourselves and those around us. But pyrite is also a stone of strength, stability, safety, and protection, showing us that true wealth doesn't come from conflict—what we take—but instead from what we create, just as true power doesn't come from harming others, but rather providing. Pyrite asks us to harness the Sacred Masculine energy within us to change the world for the better, and offer support, shelter, and aid to those in need.

3. SUNSTONE

The quintessential stone of the Sacred Masculine, sunstone is the balance to the feminine moonstone. A joy-filled crystal of light, sunstone is imbued with the qualities of personal power and magnanimous leadership. Dissolving the shame, guilt, and fear that keep us small, sunstone entreats us to step into our sovereignty, to take up space, to show the world our strength and brilliance. But just as the Sun offers its light and warmth for the good of all, without condition, so too does sunstone request that we do the same. Sunstone reminds us that to lead is to serve, and that embracing our own free will means simultaneously respecting the free will of all those around us.

4. BRONZITE

A stone of camaraderie and brotherhood, bronzite is a warm-energied stone that reminds us that we are meant to live as interconnected individuals within one community. Bronzite dissolves imposter syndrome, hesitancy, and timidity, helping us move toward our purpose with confidence and engage in what brings us joy, amplifying that positivity out into the world. In so doing, we magnetize the people most aligned for us. Bronzite is grounding and steadying, showing us how to balance our desires with the needs of our community and realign with the values of our most authentic self.

COLLECTING BY TYPE

Spiritual attributes can be a meaningful way to choose which stones to add to a collection, but historically crystal connoisseurs would seek out specimens based upon their unique characteristics or mineralogical family. Many collectors will wax poetically (and vehemently defend) whether tourmalines, calcites, or quartzes are the superior stones, while others will specialize in meteorites and tektites, garnets, fluorites, or even fossils. In the following pages we feature some of the most well-known crystalline families, as well as their geological associated properties, and the many variations you can find therein. From light-refracting calcite to useful zeolites, we'll be exploring the art of collecting crystals by type to help you discover your perfect match.

CALCITES

Ubiquitous calcite is the most common crystal on Earth after the silicate family, and can be found almost everywhere. Our ancestors valued pure calcite for jewelry, lenses, and as a maritime navigational tool, while calcite-rich stones such as marble and limestone were used as building materials, for statuary, and in medicine. But as common as it might seem, this mineral's vast variety of crystalline growth formations and full spectrum of colors means the calcite lover's collection will never be complete. Featured here are but a very small kaleidoscope of examples from this carbonate beauty.

1. OPTICAL CALCITE

Also known as Iceland spar, optical calcite is unique due to its high degree of transparency, which allows light to pass through with minimal distortion. This clear calcite typically forms angled rhombohedral crystals, which are sometimes carved into spheres to enhance its internal rainbows. It exhibits clean double refraction, capable of splitting a ray of light into two and thus creating a double image, and was used by Isaac Newton to study lightwaves. Viking sailors used Iceland spar as a navigational tool on cloudy days, as its ability to refract light allowed them to locate the Sun. Purifying and amplifying, clear calcite is well known for its ability to enhance mental clarity, vision, and focus.

2. PINK CALCITE

Pink-hued calcites fall into two categories: opaque strawberry calcite, pictured here (Mexico), and translucent rose calcite (Pakistan), which are both colored by hematite inclusions, while mangano calcite (Peru, Afghanistan) acquires its hue from manganese. Both strawberry and rose calcites tend to grow in massive or rhombohedral forms which are then carved, but mangano calcite's scalenohedral and tabular clusters are highly valued, and even carved pieces are collected for their brilliant, hot-pink fluorescence. All three resonate with the Heart chakra.

3. RED CALCITE

Red calcite's coloration is caused by hematite, or iron oxide, which either disrupts the crystalline growth to form in mass, or layers a coating on top of forming calcite, causing vivid banding. Red calcite stimulates the Root chakra, enhancing physical vitality, detoxification, stability, and motivation. This carmine crystal also supports the appreciation of our body and experiences as a physical being and is supportive in establishing healthy habits.

4. ORANGE CALCITE

Due to the presence of microcrystalline hematite inclusions, orange calcite is usually found in masses and rarely seen in crystalline form (with the notable exception of dogtooth). A popular carving medium due its soft nature, orange calcite can range from a bright, solid tangerine (Mexico) to coarsely grained pale peach (Madagascar), depending on the locality. The most distinctive feature of orange calcite is its bright and lively color, which heralds feelings of joy, creativity, and confidence. This cheery crystal also supports healthy sexuality and overcoming shame and lethargy.

5. HONEY CALCITE

Honey calcite grows in massive or rhombic formations, with hexagonal lattices, and is a translucent golden color, resembling the hue of natural honey or citrine. Found primarily in Mexico, its warm golden tones are caused by iron ions scattered within the crystal. In rarer pockets, the calcite displays double refraction. These rainbow-filled variants became known as honey optical calcite, and are highly sought after. Working with honey calcite is thought to inspire confidence, clarity of focus (especially with the optical variety), and persistence. It can help us step into our personal power and clear the blockages preventing us from receiving abundance.

6. GREEN CALCITE

Green calcite only forms when chlorite is trapped during crystallization. Sources include Mexico, for lime-green to emerald hues, and the borderlands of Pakistan and Afghanistan. When banded, green calcite is referred to as green onyx, even if this is inaccurate. Linked to the Heart chakra, green calcite activates and balances this energy center, amplifying emotional awareness, releasing emotional blockages, and easing resentment and self-directed anger.

THE SCIENCE BEHIND THE CRYSTAL

Calcite (a calcium carbonate) exhibits an array of colors and over 400 different crystal habits, the most common of which are rhombohedral, prismatic, scalenohedral, tabular, and microcrystalline boulders. This waxy stone forms in two ways: the transformation of shell and marine debris into calcite, or when water containing dissolved carbon dioxide encounters limestone or other calcium-rich rocks, which cause a chemical reaction, creating calcium carbonate molecules that over time produce calcite crystals. Calcite can develop in different environments, including caves, hydrothermal veins, and sedimentary rock layers. Found in all types of rocks, it is the basic component of limestone and marble, and used to make cement, in agricultural soil conditioners, in medicines like antacids, and as paint and whitewash. Noted for its strong birefringence, calcite has the rare ability to split a ray of light into two. Handle certain calcite varieties with care due to their Mohs 3 hardness and susceptibility to even weak acids.

7. BLUE CALCITE

Blue calcite is most often found in massive rhombohedral boulders and veins. Tones range from pale to dark blue, or even blue-green, and derive from oxidized copper impurities. Sourced from Mexico and Madagascar, variants have been found in Argentina ("blue onyx"), Pakistan ("Caribbean calcite"), and banded with dolomite in Turkey ("blue scheelite"). Paler shades support inspiration and information retention. Darker shades facilitate self-expression and can balance the Throat chakra.

8. DOGTOOTH CALCITE

Dogtooth calcite has scalenohedral (triangular) crystals with sharp terminations, resembling a dog's tooth. It ranges in color from dull gray and brown to white, red, orange, or yellow, depending on what minerals (like iron) are present. Multi-hued mariposa calcite (pictured here) and stellarbeam calcite are the most valued. This crystal removes energetic blockages hindering our ascension journey. Stellarbeam calcite is the highest vibrational form, assisting shamanic journeying, connecting with guides, and recalling past lives.

FLUORITES

Designated "the most colorful mineral in the world," vibrant fluorite can be found in every single shade of the rainbow, as well as white, black, and clear. The soft carvability of the stone and its vivid, mesmerizing patterns and hues made it a favorite ornamental stone in ancient China, Egypt, and Rome. In the 19th century, fluorite had a resurgence in popularity due to the "Blue John" variety uncovered in Derbyshire, England, which was carved to create intricate household items. This allochromatic crystal is beloved to this day by many crystal collectors, thanks to its distinctive structure, wide range of hues, and strong fluorescence.

1. COLOR-CHANGING FLUORITE

Fluorite is one of the few minerals for which specimens from numerous localities showcase the ability to change color in reaction to different lighting conditions. Pictured here is a green fluorite cluster from the Diana Maria mine, in England. This photograph was taken with incandescent lighting, but if the piece were brought outside into the sunlight it would actually turn blue! When taken back inside, the fluorite, after a short period, would return to its original green. Usually collected as specimens, rarer gem-grade pink/green or blue/ purple stones are used to make beautiful and unique pieces of jewelry. Color-changing fluorite maintains its mental-enhancing properties, but also helps us to be adaptive and promotes flexibility in our thinking.

2. BOTRYOIDAL FLUORITE

A rare growth habit for this crystal, botryoidal fluorite is almost exclusively found in India, China, and the United States. While fluorite is typically cubic or octahedral, botryoidal fluorite forms as rounded balls, crystallizing in a silica-rich liquid. As the fluorite grows, it pushes out against the silica, which in turn pushes back, forming a rounded shape. Over time, this can create a single fluorite sphere or accumulate to form a botryoidal cluster, often nestled into quartz or amethyst clusters that formed simultaneously from the silica-rich fluid. Found in golden, purple, green, or mauve-red tones, botryoidal fluorite supports slow-and-steady spiritual growth and enhances our ability to learn.

3. BLUE FLUORITE

Vivid blue is one of the most sought after of fluorite hues. While thin bands can be found in rainbow fluorite, bright cobalt saturation is rare. The azure coloration is due to trace amounts of elements, typically yttrium or copper, that substitute for calcium in the fluorite crystal structure. An excellent stone for teachers and scholars, blue fluorite helps an organized mind express itself and aids us in speaking clearly and concisely. Spiritually, blue fluorite supports the integration of our insights and the harmonization of our mental and etheric bodies.

4. RAINBOW FLUORITE

Rainbow fluorite displays an array of colors, with zones of green, clear, purple, blue, and in rarer cases, yellow or pink. This polychromatic variety forms as mineral solutions with differing inclusions crystallize in layers, creating banding patterns of varying colors and thicknesses. Key sources are China and Mexico, where it grows in hydrothermal veins. It can be carved into almost any shape, including towers or spheres, or as cabochons for jewelry. Due to its color combinations, this crystal is thought to resonate with multiple chakras and is useful for opening the Third Eye, enhancing spiritual abilities and helping with memory and focus.

5. WINDOW FLUORITE

Window fluorite gives us a peek into the growth process of this interesting formation. The fluorite of this specimen develops in multiple stages, either as individual crystals, as shown here, or in clusters. First, a clear cubic fluorite forms; then a new color of fluorite is introduced, which encases the initial crystal along the edges or corners, causing a "frame" or "window" that allows us to see through or into the fluorite. Metaphysically, window fluorite increases mental clarity, helps us view our situation with a clear perspective, and, like all fluorites, aids in the retention of information.

6. CUBIC FLUORITE

Cubic (6-sided) fluorite forms from lower temperature hydrothermal fluids, while fluorite formed from higher temperature fluids tends to occur as octahedral (8-sided) crystals. Found as clusters, high-grade, single-cube specimens have been sourced in Spain, China, Russia, and the USA. The largest single crystal of fluorite so far documented was a cube of around 7ft (2.1m)! Colors vary widely across the spectrum, the most common being purple and green. Cubic fluorite enhances mental clarity and focus and aids well-thought-out decisions. This formation in particular is also considered mentally protective.

THE SCIENCE BEHIND THE CRYSTAL

Pure fluorite crystals are actually colorless; the sheer variety of colors are due to minor elemental substitutions/impurities in fluorite's chemical composition that either tint the crystal, or change its color in response to radiation in the environment. Fluorite forms through hydrothermal activity, occurring in limestone veins, hydrothermal deposits, and in granite pegmatites. It was, and still is, used as a flux in metal smelting to remove impurities, and in a variety of chemical and ceramic processes. It is also a source of fluorine, and used as a lens material for both infrared and ultraviolet wavelengths. One of fluorite's more unusual properties is that it fluoresces under ultraviolet light due to trace amounts of europium. The term "fluorescence" was named after this very special mineral.

7. SNOWFLAKE FLUORITE

Aptly named snowflake fluorite (or feather fluorite), this soft green or deep purple fluorite contains constrasting, delicate, white aragonite dendrites that seem to swirl within. This microcrystalline variety grows almost exclusively in hydrothermal pockets in China, and is typically polished and carved to showcase its dendrites. Metaphysically, this uncommon fluorite helps to harmonize the Crown, Third Eye, and Heart centers, clear energetic blockages, and invite calmness and serenity.

8. SILKY FLUORITE

An opaque microcrystalline fluorite hailing solely from China. What catalyzes the formation of this Chinese opaque fluorite is unknown: some think it is due to quartz or calcite inclusions, some to compression as the fluorite grows. Occasionally green, silky fluorite is usually found in bands of light lavender to dark purples, and is only ever purchasable carved or polished. Energetically, it is very gentle, so ideal for the bedside or in children's bedrooms to invite sweet dreams—it can help quieten our minds and support relaxed meditation.

FELDSPARS

The iridescent shimmer, opalescent play of color, and rainbow flash of feldspar crystals have inspired and fascinated humans for thousands of years. An important member of the silicate family, feldspars are the most common mineral on the planet, comprising over half of the Earth's crust, and have even been found as distantly as the Moon and far-flung meteorites. It's no wonder these beauties are often associated with spirits, satellites, and stars.

1. AMAZONITE
Microcline Alkali Feldspar
While microcline feldspars come in a variety of colors (white, cream, yellow, pink, and red), it is the teal and blue varieties that are most well known. Named amazonite after the waters of the Amazon River, this shimmering semi-precious stone is valued as an aid to sincere communication, emotional honesty, compassion, and the courage to live authentically.

2. CLEAVELANDITE
Sodium Feldspar
Cleavelandite is the gemmy, plated variety of albite. Often found in pegmatites, cleavelandite can also form beautiful specimens. These delicate-looking blades are typically translucent and clear, although icy blue-tinted clusters are particularly prized by collectors. Cleavelandite is said to help us through challenging circumstances or times of profound change, shifting our focus to the possibilities that can arise out of difficult situations.

3. MOONSTONE (mixed colors)
Alkali Feldspar
Moonstone is a common name used to classify any feldspar that shows a white or silvery iridescence, and can be a member of the orthoclase, anorthoclase or sanidine subfamilies. Believed by the ancients to have been created by drops of crystallized moonlight, moonstone is imbued with the energy of the Moon: stimulating our intuition, strengthening the Sacred Feminine within, and, like its namesake, protecting and guiding us during the long hours of the night.

4. SUNSTONE
Oligoclase Plagioclase Feldspar

The counterbalance to moonstone, this reddish-orange, flashing stone encapsulates the benevolent leadership, courage, vitality, and joy associated with the Sun. Naturally colorless, white, yellow, or even green, minute inclusions of hematite create its recognizable color, which, viewed through the feldspar, sparkle and flash in direct light. Notable localities for high-grade sunstone are India, Tanzania, and Oregon, in the USA.

5. LABRADORITE
Plagioclase Feldspar

Labradorite is associated with pure magic: a dark stone flashing brilliant colors. The hues aren't actually in the crystal, as this feldspar has very fine, tightly compacted layers, which refract and reflect light, creating a polychromatic display. Blue, teal, and yellow flash are more common than the popular pinks, coppers, and purples. It is found in Madagascar and Canada, but the finest comes from Finland (spectrolite).

THE SCIENCE BEHIND THE CRYSTAL

Feldspars are more than just flashy stones. The crystals featured here are the most well-known, and typically popular thanks to their Schiller effect (shimmer or flash), but over 20 different members of this family exist, each prized not just for their beauty, but also their functionality. Feldspars are a main component of granite, a staple in glass, ceramic, and paint production, and commonly featured in buildings, home decor, and monuments.

Geologically, feldspar's crystalline structure is composed of aluminum, silicon, and oxygen. This mineralogical family is then subdivided into two to four main groups:

- Alkali feldspars, which contain potassium.
- Plagioclase feldspars, which contain calcium.
- Sodium feldspars, which contain sodium, and are considered to be both plagioclase and alkali.
- Barium feldspars, which are often considered a subgroup of the alkali feldspars because the potassium has been replaced by barium.

6. RAINBOW MOONSTONE
Plagioclase Feldspar

Typically flashing bright blue, rainbow moonstone is named for the full-spectrum Schiller effect (see page 141) that can occur in rarer examples of this beautiful stone. Geologically speaking, rainbow moonstone is actually a white variety of labradorite, but its association as a moonstone has been ongoing for thousands of years, with its properties of magic and protection closely aligned to its cousins. Gem-grade cabachons are often utilized in jewelry, while mid-grade deposits with freckles of flash and black tourmaline inclusions are transformed into spheres, towers, or carvings.

7. GARNIERITE
Nickle Ore in Feldspar (various)

While garnierite technically refers to the green nickel ore found embedded within the crystal, the name is colloquially used to signify garnierite in feldspars, (pictured here). Garnierite is sometimes called "green moonstone" due to its shimmer and occasional blue flash, but the ore within is more closely related to serpentine, and it shouldn't be confused with Himalayan green or parrot (green and pink) moonstone. Energetically, this nickel and feldspar combination is one of regeneration, supportive for healing the heart, our physical bodies, our planet, and even our bank accounts.

COPPER-BEARING CRYSTALS

Copper is the metal of connection. A conduit for energy, both electric and thermal, as well as spiritual, copper facilitates the channeling of higher frequencies into the physical world and the communication of thoughts, ideas, and emotions to others. Copper-infused crystals reflect this, and have been valued as sacred stones since ancient times. From the emotionally creative energies of chrysocolla to the profound wisdom emanating from azurite, these beautiful crystals hold the potential to illuminate our inner truth so we can honestly connect with others.

1. MALACHITE
Copper(II) Carbonate

The brilliant, swirling, banded greens of malachite have been favored as a cosmetic, paint pigment, and ornamental stone for thousands of years. Created by weathering of copper ores, malachite can be botryoidal, fibrous, or even grow as stalactites. Often found with azurite, prominent malachite localities include central Africa, the North American Southwest, Israel, Australia, and France. Metaphysically, malachite is a heart-protector, absorbing and transforming pain so we can heal.

2. CHRYSOCOLLA
Hydrous Copper Phyllosilicate

Chrysocolla is a fascinating copper stone in that, as a combination of copper, aluminum, silicon, and water, it has a variable composition. With high levels of silicon, chrysocolla becomes known as gem silica or chrysocolla chalcedony and has a Mohs hardness of 7, while lower levels means the stone actually lacks a distinct crystalline structure. Instead of growing crystals, chrysocolla often forms crusts, coatings, nodules, rivers, or botryoidal masses in association with other minerals. Its blues and cyans make it a popular jewelry gemstone. Chrysocolla helps us express our emotions with clarity and honesty. It also facilitates teaching and creative expression, particularly in music.

3. SHATTUCKITE
Copper Silicate Hydroxide

First discovered in 1915 at the Shattuck Mine of Arizona, shattuckite is a rare secondary copper silicate crystal that is often the result of transformed malachite. Found in varying formations because it replaces the molecules of other minerals, shattuckite forms as long or short fibrous crystalline sprays, botryoidal balls, or as a granular mass in light and dark blues, or beautiful bold turquoise. Shattuckite assists in spiritual communication, helping us receive messages from our guides, angels, ancestors, and Higher Self, and is particularly beneficial for channeling. It's also supportive in balancing the Throat chakra and enhancing our ability to recognize and speak our Truth.

4. AZURITE
Copper (II) Carbonate

Named for its signature color, azurite is an oxidized copper mineral that has been used as a paint pigment for almost 5,000 years. Able to grow as fine crystals, druzy, nodular, botryoidal "blueberries," or in granular masses, azurite is actually a molecularly unstable crystal and in nature will slowly transform into malachite. Many paintings that utilized azurite as the source for blue pigment show a greenish tint today due to this effect. Fine specimens are most often sourced from Arizona, France, Mexico, Namibia, and the Ural Mountains. Metaphysically, azurite is associated with wisdom, mental processes, intuition, insight, and spiritual awakening.

5. CUPRITE
Copper (I) Oxide

A red copper ore nicknamed "ruby copper" due to its coloring, cuprite is a secondary mineral, meaning it forms only after copper sulfide grows and then oxidizes. It usually grows with sister stones like shattuckite, but can also crystallize into well-defined cubic or octahedral gems that would be highly valued as jewelry but for the brittle and soft nature of the mineral. Cuprite is another Divine Feminine crystal, and believed to connect us with the deep resonance of the Earth. Grounding cuprite stimulates life force energy, promoting a sense of stability, security and strength.

6. DIOPTASE
Copper (II) Cyclosilicate

A bold green, miners initially thought dioptase was a type of emerald when it was first discovered. Although the stunning stone is too soft to carve, this rare rhombohedral or prismatic crystal is still highly sought after, with fine specimen clusters most often sourced from Namibia, Republic of Congo, and Kazakhstan. Dioptase commonly grows with chrysocolla, and is often associated with emotional healing, forgiveness, trauma-recovery, and heart-centered energies. It's believed to promote compassion, both for ourselves and for others.

7. ATACAMITE
Copper (II) Halide

Atacamite is an uncommon stone found in oxidized copper deposits amid the arid landscapes of Chile, the North American Southwest, Australia, and China, and in deep volcanic vents on the seabed. Forming dark green, prismatic, or tabular crystals, it can also occur as fibrous or botryoidal combinations with cuprite, malachite, linarite, celedonite, or chrysocolla. Since it is caused by oxidized copper, samples of atacamite have even been found on ancient copper coins and the Statue of Liberty. Energetically, atacamite is associated with physical renewal and emotional healing.

THE SCIENCE BEHIND THE CRYSTAL

Copper was one of the first metals to be consistently mined, over 11,000 years ago. It's soft and malleable, easy to manipulate into jewelry and tools, and its use brought humanity out of the Stone Age. In antiquity, our ancestors found copper-bearing crystals, typically low on the Mohs hardness scale, easier to carve and grind than silicates like quartz, and that, combined with their vivid colors, made these stones popular for ornamentation and pigments. Over 150 different minerals contain copper, as do around 25 well-known gemstones, like those listed here as well as larimar, turquoise, ajoite, smithsonite, Oregon sunstone, and Paraiba tourmaline.

Copper imparts a wide range of colors to its crystals which is dependent on the oxidation process while the stone forms: bold blues, bright teals, and deep greens are common, although visceral reds, browns, and strong blacks are seen as well. The copper inclusions can influence crystal growth patterns and introduce zones of higher conductivity.

The high demand for copper worldwide means mining for the metal is extensive, with many of these minerals ground up or leached for the copper they contain. Today, many of the copper crystals are found near mines, or are by-products of the mining process.

ZEOLITES

The hardest working of any crystal family, zeolites (both natural and synthetic) are utilized in more commercial processes than any other stone. Distinguished by their open, microscopic lattice structure that is able to readily assimilate and hold other molecules, zeolites can act as an adsorbent, sieve, and catalyst. These unsung heroes of industry almost all resonate metaphysically with the upper chakras, and serve as high vibrational guides and meditation allies.

1. HEULANDITE
Tetrahedral Zeolite
Heulandite forms as delicate, pearly layers of rhombic prisms or wedges, as can be seen here underneath the larger stilbite clusters. Normally clear or white, various inclusions such as hematite or celedonite (a dark green mica) can color the mineral pink, red, green, orange, brown, or yellow. Interestingly, heulandite isn't a single crystal but a series of five variations, each with a slightly different molecular structure, although all visually identical. Heulandite can stimulate and enhance our intuition and psychic perception, assist us in developing clairvoyant or clairaudient abilities, and support expansion at the soul level.

2. STILBITE
Tetrahedral Zeolite
Stilbite is recognizable by its peach to salmon-pink coloring, and its wheat-sheaf or fanlike growth habit. It can be most often found growing with fellow zeolites or apophyllite. Useful for dreamwork, including dream recall and lucid dreaming, stilbite also promotes expansive and consistent meditation practices and reconnection with our most loving and truest sense of self.

3. NATROLITE
Fibrous Zeolite
Clear, white, pink, or gray, natrolite typically forms slender, needle-like, prismatic crystals and can also occur as radiating clusters. The name "natrolite" is derived from the Greek words *natri* (sodium) and *lithos* (stone), indicating its sodium-rich composition. In the specimen pictured above, the white, spray-like formation is natrolite and the orange crystal is chabazite. Natrolite is thought to have a calming and soothing energy that can help balance and stabilize thoughts and emotions, reduce stress and anxiety, and help us to align with our higher purpose.

4. SCOLECITE
Fibrous Zeolite

Known for its delicate, white spray formations, scolecite can also be polished and carved into shimmering, wing-patterned palm stones and spheres, as shown here. Scolecite is used in meditation practices to enhance inner stillness, promote a state of deep relaxation, and facilitate communication with spiritual guides or higher dimensional beings.

5. CHABAZITE
Tabular Zeolite

Chabazite is a rare pseudo-cubic zeolite, with crystals that are often twinned. Sporting a beautiful range of colors, including white, pink, orange, brown, green, or yellow, chabazite naturally grows with fellow zeolites such as natrolite, but is often replicated in laboratories for industrial use. Metaphysically, white chabazite is believed to help mental clarity and mindfulness, and support understanding of spiritual precepts, while pink, orange, and yellow chabazite promote self-awareness and the release of destructive habits.

6. THOMSONITE
Fibrous Zeolite

One of the rarest zeolites, thomsonite falls into two subcategories, one with calcite and the rarer version with strontium inclusions. Usually found in rounded "puffball" shapes, thomsonite can also be polished into beautiful specimens for jewelry. This stone is simultaneously associated with grounding, nurturing, and protective energies, as well as spiritual growth.

7. APOPHYLLITE
Fluorapophyllite • Hydroxyapophyllite

Although it is often associated with zeolites, apophyllite is actually its own mineralogical family, subdivided into five different species. Zeolites and apophyllites are in many ways sister crystals, and can almost always be found growing together in beautiful pyramidal or tabular arrangements. Usually clear, apophyllite can also be found in green, pink, violet, black, blue, or golden hues. Apophyllite is known for connecting with guides and the Higher Self, as well as raising the vibration of any space it's in.

THE SCIENCE BEHIND THE CRYSTAL

Zeolites are geologically aluminosilicate minerals, formed through the slow interaction of volcanic rock, ash, and alkaline groundwater. The name zeolite, which translates to "boiling stone," is derived from its unique ability to steam when heated due to the release of trapped water molecules. This fascinating stone's microporous framework of aluminum, oxygen, and silicon with alkali metals grants it a remarkable capacity for molecular absorption and release.

The unique crystalline structure renders zeolites invaluable in a diverse range of industrial applications, from water purification, to catalytic processes, to dietary supplements, to kitty litter. Zeolites have been used by NASA to grow plants in space, and they are today being explored for their potential use in environmental remediation projects, including cleaning up contaminated sites and safely storing and disposing of radioactive waste. There are over 40 types of naturally occurring zeolites, but laboratory-grown ones number over 150 different structural frameworks.

TEKTITES

Imagine: a meteorite comes screaming through our atmosphere and slams into the surface of the Earth. The heat and energy released upon impact instantaneously melt the terrestrial rock that's been hit, as well as the surface of the meteorite itself: these melted globs are thrown back up into the atmosphere, fuse, and then plummet back down to Earth, miles away from the initial impact. The impact and freefall happen so fast—the melted silica cools so quickly—that it doesn't have time to crystallize. Thus are tektites, meteoric impact glasses, born. These incredible mineraloids, themselves changed in an instant, are tools of rapid transformation and spiritual expansion.

1. MOLDAVITE

Green moldavite formed about 15 million years ago during a meteorite impact in Germany. Largely from the Czech Republic, it is named for the Moldau (Vltava) River, where the first specimens were found. All moldavite is characterized by its pitted, etched surfaces, but the flowery or hedgehog-like specimens are the most highly prized. This meteoric glass may be faceted for jewelry or carved into skulls or ornaments, but these can be easy to imitate, so source from a good dealer. A potent stone, physical effects like heart palpitations, headaches, and jitters may occur without a grounding crystal. It is a tool of transformation, rapid spiritual growth, and enhanced psychic abilities. It is believed to facilitate communication with other beings and dimensional traveling during meditation.

2. LIBYAN DESERT GLASS

Libyan desert glass is an impactite found in the deserts of Libya and Egypt, created when a meteor hit the Sahara Desert about 29 million years ago. The force of the impact caused the sands to melt at temperatures in excess of 3,000°F. Made of almost pure silica, golden tektite was knapped by Neolithic people to make tools. The ancient Egyptians revered it as a sacred stone associated with the Sun and expertly carved this meteoric glass into jewelry and amulets, such as the scarab beetle centered in Pharaoh Tutankhamun's breastplate. Libyan desert glass increases the potency of our will, supporting our ability to step into our divine ability to manifest and create. Like all tektites and impactites, it's believed to help us connect to extraterrestrial guides, as well as ancient Akashic wisdom.

4. COLOMBIANITE (PSEUDO-TEKTITE)

Colombianite is what's known as a pseudo-tektite, along with saffordites from Arizona and agnimanites from Indonesia. While for many decades these were believed to be tektites, they are, in fact, a rare obsidian formed by an ancient volcanic blast so hot and powerful that silica was projected high into the atmosphere where it fell back down to Earth, hence the similar appearance to tektites. Most obsidian is young, geologically speaking, and rarely older than 5-20 million years, as it is relatively unstable and will eventually transform into stone or crystal.

Colombianite, on the other hand, is about 30 million years old and has retained its molecular composition. Colombianite, known locally as *piedra rayo*, or "lightning stone," usually has a small button or rounded shape and is found in the Cauca River area of Columbia. Believed to be sacred to the Muisca people, Colombianite is said to connect us to the divine and support communication with ancestors, deities, and guides. Simultaneously high vibrational and grounding, Colombianite is associated with spiritual journeying, healing, transformation, and change.

THE SCIENCE BEHIND THE CRYSTAL

Although similar to volcanic glass (obsidian), tektites are differentiated by their low water content and an abundance of lechatelierite, a silica mineraloid (non-crystal) that can only be produced under very high temperatures or pressure beyond the norm for our planet. Tetktites fall into four main categories:

Splashform: Round, dumbbell, teardrop, or onion-shaped; often pitted and grooved.
Aerodynamic: Button-shaped, with a smooth exterior caused by a solidified tektite thrown so high that it melted a second time as it re-entered the Earth's atmosphere.
Muong-Nong: Larger, layered tektites, pocketed with other minerals.
Microtektites: Miniscule splashforms typically found under water.

There are smaller strewn fields (where tektites or meteorites fall from a single meteoric impact) in North America, Central America, and Russia, but the most well known are:

The Central European Strewn Field: 15 million years old; source of moldavite
The Ivory Coast Strewn Field: 1 million years old; source of ivorites
The North American Strewn Field: 35 million years old; source of brownish-black bediasites (Texas) and green georgiaites (Georgia)
The Australasian Strewn Field: 788,000 years old; source of various indochinites

In addition, desert "impactites" exist, such as Libyan desert glass from the Sahara Desert, Darwin glass from the desert of Tasmania, or the rare Atacama desert glass from Chile.

3. INDOCHINITE

The youngest and largest of the four major strewn fields (see Box, opposite) was caused by a meteor hitting Southeast Asia only 788,000 years ago, scattering tektites across Asia, the Pacific Islands, Australia, Antarctica, and the Indian and Pacific oceans. From this one meteoric impact we have numerous varieties of tektites, including thailandites, phillipinites, Vietnamese Muong-Nong, the flying saucer/button-shaped australites, black Tibetan tektites, and more, all of which are collectively known as indochinites. Each type is beautifully unique and exudes a distinct energetic signature, with many used as sacred talismans by the Indigenous peoples of their respective localities. All are guides and allies in the acceleration of our spiritual evolution.

COLLECTING BY UNIQUE FEATURE

The wide world of crystals and minerals is an enthralling place, with geological marvels and oddities that perplex us just as easily as they might fascinate. In this section, we focus on the unique and the interesting: stones that surreally glow in the dark, contain hidden treasures, or have undergone dramatic transformations of their very own. Many professional collectors choose to focus entirely on these distinctive specimens, but even if you typically select your crystals based on their spiritual associations or healing properties, the stones here make a beautiful and intriguing addition to any collection.

SPECIAL QUARTZ FORMATIONS

Quartz, the most prolific and versatile of crystals, can grow in a variety of formations depending on locality and conditions. Beyond the normal hexagonal point or geode we correlate with quartz, each of these formations has its own unique associations and is a testament to nature's artistry.

Also pictured: Tabular Quartz (8)

1. ELESTIAL QUARTZ
Skeletal Quartz • Alligator Quartz
Elestial quartz has a unique pebbled, etched, or layered appearance that arises from smaller quartz crystals overgrowing the surfaces of larger ones, often forming "windows." Metaphysically, high-vibrational elestial serves as a potent ally for meditation and facilitates a profound connection with our higher selves.

2. CATHEDRAL QUARTZ
Lightbrary Quartz
Cathedral quartz is characterized by smaller terminations rising parallel from a larger central point, creating the appearance of a cathedral or spire-like structure. It is also known as Lightbrary quartz due to its association with the Akashic Records, and is believed to be a crystalline key to the "library of light." An uncommon formation of spiritual enlightenment, cathedral quartz is thought to hold the energy of sacred spaces and universal wisdom.

3. LEMURIAN QUARTZ
Lemurian Seed Crystal • Lemurian Star Seed Crystals
Lemurian quartz has a unique growth pattern featuring horizontal striations or "barcode-like" markings along its sides. Also referred to as "staircase" or "ladder" formations, some believe these lines are encoded with information from the mythological civilization of Lemuria, a heart-based utopia that existed as a counterpoint to Atlantis. By meditating or running fingers along the barcodes, it's thought we can access the wisdom stored within to heal and expand ourselves and the collective.

4. RECORD KEEPERS
Recorder Quartz • Record-Keeping Quartz

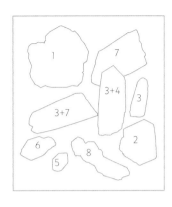

Record keepers are triangular markings or indentations on the crystal face, either upright (traditional) or upside down (trigon). These are said to store the wisdom of the mythological civilization of Atlantis, seeded around the world for when we need them most. Sourced from sacred localities like the Himalayas and found on high-vibrational crystals like Herkimer diamonds, Nirvana quartz, and Lemurian quartz, record keepers connect us to our past, present, future.

5. DOUBLE-TERMINATED QUARTZ
DT Quartz • Double-Point Quartz
Double-terminated quartz crystals form with pointed (terminated) ends on both sides due to their unique growth process. Although dual terminations can be carved, naturally occurring DTs are rare, more valuable, and have a greater potency. This quartz is a powerful tool for energy balancing and amplification during body layouts, crystal gridding, or in ritual work since it can channel and project energy in dual directions, making it useful for facilitating harmonious energy flow and achieving balance and alignment.

6. SCEPTER
Scepter Crystal
This has a distinct growth pattern, with a small quartz crystal crowned by a larger central crystal, creating a scepter-like formation. This quartz is linked to spiritual authority, inner strength, self-empowerment, and transformation. The prominent central point symbolizes qualities of leadership, along with the power to concentrate and guide energy with precision.

7. TWIN
Quartz Twinning
Twin quartz is not a specific quartz variety, but a phenomenon where two separate quartz crystals grow in a symmetrical or mirror-image formation while sharing the same base. This occurs when one crystal splits, or two crystals with the same crystallographic orientation come into contact in their growth process. Twinning results in a variety of forms: Twin Flames (twinned crystals with a shared base pointing away from each other to create a "V"), Tantric Twin (twinned crystals of similar height and size, like the 7 on the left), and Mother and Child (crystals with one smaller than the other, like the 7 at the top right).

QUARTZ INCLUSIONS

The inclusions found within quartz are vast and varied, ranging from microscopic minerals like hematite, which tint the normally clear crystal distinctive hues, to specimens such as pyrite, mica, or amphibole that have become encased and protected by the silicate surrounding it. The quartz both amplifies the properties of the inclusions within and is itself transformed by each synergistic partnership.

Also pictured: Lepidocrocite in Quartz (9)

1. PHANTOM QUARTZ
Ghost Quartz
Phantom quartz derives its name from the spectral visage of inner "phantoms." These faint outlines showcase earlier growth stages within the larger crystal, each leaving behind a subtle to distinct imprint. This is interpreted as a poignant symbol of continuous growth and evolution. It serves as a reminder that progress is an ongoing, ever-unfolding journey, and supports our ability to access our younger selves and past lives in order to fully heal.

2. RUTILATED QUARTZ
Venus' Hair Quartz • Angel Hair Quartz
Rutile-included quartz is highly sought after, especially fine specimens with exceptional clarity that display rutilated starburst patterns. Rutile, a titanium dioxide mineral, will often develop first, and later become encased by liquid silica that becomes quartz, preserving the golden, copper, red, or silver needle-like threads within. Rutilated quartz resonates with the Solar Plexus and Crown chakras, and is one of the most aligned crystals for manifestation.

3. CHLORITE-INCLUDED QUARTZ
Garden Quartz • Lodolite • Shaman Quartz
Chlorite is group of common phyllosilicate minerals found in metamorphic and igneous rocks. Upon its inclusion in quartz, however, chlorite's magic becomes clear. Appearing as worlds within worlds, chlorite can be used as a meditation tool to deepen our connections with the natural world, facilitate our physical healing, and, in its phantom form, support our emotional recovery.

4. AMPHIBOLE QUARTZ
Angel Phantom Quartz
Hailing solely from Brazil, amphibole quartz is renowned for its swirls of red, pink, orange, and occasionally silvery-blue coloring due to the infusion of diverse amphibole minerals like actinolite and tremolite. Amphibole quartz is useful for meditation and serves as a conduit for communication with higher realms.

5. HEMATOID QUARTZ
Hematite-Included Quartz • Pink Quartz • Tangerine Quartz • Golden Healer
When microscopic particles of hematite (an iron-oxide mineral) are present, it can turn quartz red, orange, yellow, pink, gray, or black, depending on the conditions in which it is introduced, each with distinct metaphysical associations. Samadhi quartz, pictured here, is a rare variety of pink quartz from the Himalayas.

6. AVENTURINE
Mica-Included Quartz • Tanzberry
Named after sparkling, copper-flecked glass first made in Italy, aventurine's glitter is completely natural and derived from mica inclusions. The most well known is green aventurine, which is colored by the green-hued fuschite mica, but blue aventurine and raspberry aventurine (pictured here) are also popular. Aventurine's spiritual properties vary depending on the type of mica in the aventurine, as well as other minerals that might be present. Raspberry aventurine is sweet and soothing, an emotionally healing stone that helps us reflect within and release blockages that may be keeping our heart closed.

7. DUMORTIERITE QUARTZ
Blue Quartz
Beautiful, bold dumortierite strikingly layers within quartz, as seen here. When enough microcrystalline dumortierite is present, however, it can stain quartz entirely blue, which then becomes known as blue quartz, or, if mica is also present, blue aventurine. Fine clear quartz specimens and clusters with delicate, distinct tendrils are highly sought after. Dumortierite quartz supports self-discipline, patience, focus, and mental acuity.

8. CARBON-INCLUDED QUARTZ
Black Quartz
Found in high-vibrational, naturally double-terminated crystals such as Herkimers and Tibetan quartz, carbon-included quartz is simultaneously purifying and protective, and contributes to an expanded consciousness.

ENHYDROS

Enhydros, meaning "water within," are crystals in which fluids such as water or petroleum have became encased within the mineral. Encapsulating a fragment of the Earth's ancient history, some enhydros are over 56 million years old, and can offer geologists clues to our planet's ever-evolving terrain. Elestials, Herkimer diamonds, selenite, agates, and silicate varieties such as clear quartz, smoky quartz, and amethyst are the most common fluid-included crystals.

HYDROTHERMALLY ETCHED

High upon the steepest mountain slopes and deep within the Earth, mineral-rich waters flow, alchemizing the crystals with which they come into contact. These dissolution crystals are hydrothermally etched and display intricate patterns and textures that are shaped by this intimate interplay between mineral and liquid.

1. AGATE ENHYDROS
Agate enhydros form as silica-rich water filters through volcanic rock, shaping layers of deposited crystal that create a cavity in which the water becomes trapped. Oftentimes, a sloshing sound can be heard when the stone is shaken and the liquid within can be seen when it is held up to the light. Metaphysically, agate enhydro is purifying, balancing, and replenishing, making it an ideal ally when we wish to cleanse toxicity from our body, release density from our energetic field, and revitalize our souls.

2. QUARTZ ENHYDROS
Enhydro-filled quartz takes shape as water becomes enclosed within the developing crystal or seeps in along healing crystal fractures. Clear quartz is already a powerfully adaptive and versatile crystal, able to hold within and amplify programmed intentions. Water, too, shifts and changes, while it is also believed to hold memory and energetic patterns—it is after all the liquified form of ice, which, geologically speaking, is technically a crystal. When these two mutable intention-keepers combine, the results are palpable in their ability to manifest, as well as support, our capacity to adapt and transform.

3. AMETHYST ENHYDROS
While amethyst is honored for its peaceful nature and the spiritual support it offers, the addition of enhydro inclusions augments its ability to balance our thoughts and emotions. The primordial waters within facilitate our ability to plumb the depths of our mind and heart to uncover hidden truths, and aid in accessing the spiritual wisdom gleaned from ancient guides and our past lives. Amethyst enhydros are most often found in Vera Cruz and skeletal varieties, as well as in Namibian and Himalayan localities.

4. NIRVANA QUARTZ/ICE QUARTZ
Discovered in 2012, this rare and beautifully "scarred," clear or pink quartz is a type of growth-interference crystal, worn away by expanding and retreating glaciers over millions of years high in the Himalayas. Just as they bear the marks of their experiences, so they reflect back to us that our own story, although painful at times, is actually the path for our own expansive enlightenment. Many Nirvana quartzes feature traditional and trigonic record keepers, which are especially prized, and bespeak the importance of inner acceptance, wisdom, and spiritual awakening.

5. HYDRO-ETCHED MORGANITE
Beryls, such as aquamarine and morganite, can occasionally undergo a distinct etching process as slightly acidic water runs down the crystal either during or after its formation, leading to unique and visually intriguing features across the surface of the stone. Morganite is energetically connected to themes of Universal Love and compassion, with the "etched" appearance a poignant symbol of the transmutive healing journey we experience when we move from feeling diminished by fear or heartbreak to embracing a perspective of love.

6. HYDRO-ETCHED AMETHYST
Hydro-etched amethyst first forms as intact, recognizable purple quartz points. In rare circumstances and unique localities, however, near-boiling or sulfuric water is introduced, slowly etching away at the crystal's sides and faces, creating grooves, twists, crannies, and intricate patterns. Having undergone its own transformation, hydro-etched amethyst is an ally during transformative times within our own lives.

ORGANIC GEMSTONES

Organic gemstones are the fascinating intersection of living, breathing beings and our crystalline cousins. Some gemstones are created by the animal itself through biomineralization; others only as flora and fauna transform in their entirety after death, slowly becoming stone as each of their cells is replaced by minerals. Many of these fossils tell vivid stories of ancient eras, offering a tangible link to the past and allowing us to glimpse the world as it once was.

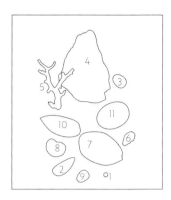

Also pictured: Ammonite (8), Trilobite (9), Orthoceras (10), Kambaba Jasper (11)

1. PEARL
Pearl

An exquisite organic gemstone cultivated through the remarkable process of biomineralization, pearls are found around the world in a spectrum of muted, shimmering colors. Both fresh and saltwater bivalve mollusks meticulously layer two versions of calcium carbonate—calcite and a plateleted form of aragonite—around a grain of sand or irritant as a means of protection, resulting in a gleaming pearl held deep within its body. Pearls are believed to deepen our intuition, help us overcome uncomfortable situations by shifting our perspective, align with our inner wisdom, and also enhance our connection with the element of water and the Sacred Feminine.

2. AMBER
Amber

Beloved by humans as jewelry and used as medicine since Neolithic times, amber is created through the fossilization of tree resin. Not to be confused with the much younger copal, or hardened resin, amber ranges in age between 15 and 320 million years old, with important localities in Dominican Republic, Myanmar, the Mediterranian, and the Baltic. Metaphysically, amber is closely linked with healing, protection, and vitality, and exudes a warm, nurturing energy associated with the sun.

3. JET
Lignite

Jet, while often mistaken for a mineral, is actually a form of lignite, a mineraloid precursor to coal. It originates from the transformation of woody remains through a process of carbonization that spans millions of years. This natural alchemy yields a smooth, compact material capable of achieving a brilliant polish. Jet holds a reputation as a protective stone, esteemed for its remarkable capacity to absorb, stabilize, and transmute negative energy.

4. PETRIFIED WOOD
Fossilized Wood

Petrified wood, with its whorls and rings of patterned stone, is a natural phenomenon that occurs through the slow substitution of organic matter by minerals. This can lead to quartz, agate, or opal assuming the form of the original wood structure, resulting in a crystal that visually resembles wood grain. Petrified wood is a stone of grounding, transformation, patience, and ancient wisdom, and offers us a profound opportunity to connect with nature.

5. CORAL
Precious Coral • Red Coral

Coral is primarily constituted of calcium carbonate, the same building blocks as seashells, pearls, calcite, and aragonite. It arises due to the collective endeavors of marine polyps, which make the mineral to build sturdy exoskeletons, creating branching or mound-like formations. Red coral, in particular, had been valued as a gemstone for centuries, although overharvesting and climate change has led to its decline. Associated with royalty, vitality, wisdom, confidence, and happiness, red coral is considered the most auspicious of all corals.

6. AGATIZED SHELL
Agate Shell • Fossilized Shell

Agatized shells are born when the original calcium carbonate shell undergoes gradual substitution by silica-rich fluids. The outcome is a shell fashioned entirely from agate. Agatized shells are considered protective, especially when traveling over water. Emotionally, these little talismans are soothing and steadying for the watery depths of the heart, helping us explore our emotions in a way that feels safe.

7. MOTHER-OF-PEARL
Nacre

With its iridescent allure, mother-of-pearl has long been cherished in jewelry and mosaics. The interplay of aragonite and conchiolin forms the inner lining of mollusk shells, imparting their distinctive shimmer. In addition, mother-of-pearl is thought to attract prosperity, soothe stress, offer protection, and heighten intuition.

FLUORESCENT MINERALS

While crystals can be found in almost every shade under the sun, some minerals hold a secret that comes alive only when exposed to the magic of ultraviolet light. Produced by low- and high-pressure mercury arcs with wavelengths of 254 nanometers (shortwave) to 320–400 nanometers (longwave), ultraviolet light illuminates the hidden colors of fluorescent crystals, revealing a world that seems to belong in another dimension.

Note: While longwave UV (blacklight) is relatively safe, shortwave UV can irritate the eyes and burn the skin, so UV goggles should be worn to prevent eye damage.

1. AMBER
Longwave, Shortwave

Formed through the fossilization of resin from ancient trees, amber fluoresces white, blue, green, or yellow depending on locality. Associated with our ancestral lineages and the warmth of the Sun, amber can support our physical vitality, help us reconnect to genetic memory, and enable us to embody joy.

2. ARAGONITE
Longwave, Shortwave

Aragonite is another form of calcium carbonate, the same as calcite, but features a different molecular structure and typically fluoresces white or blue-green. Aragonite's metaphysical properties depend on its coloring and locality, but it's often utilized for clearing and raising vibrational frequencies.

3. CALCITE
Longwave, Shortwave

Found in almost all the colors of the rainbow, calcite's fluorescence depends on the mineral inclusions that lend their hue. Manganese causes calcite to fluoresce hot pink, while other varieties can appear red, blue, white, green, or orange.

4. CORUNDUM (RUBY AND SAPPHIRE)
Longwave, Shortwave

A well-known fluorescer, one of ruby's distinctive characteristics is its bright red glow under longwave light. Sapphire of varying hues can also glow red or yellow as long as iron levels within the stone are low enough not to counteract the UV. Ruby evokes passion and grounded embodiment, while sapphire instills wisdom, mental clarity, and focus.

5. DOLOMITE
Shortwave

Fluorescing pale yellow to bright red, dolomite is believed to bring stability and support through life's twists and turns.

6. FLUORITE
Longwave, Shortwave

The crystal from which fluorescence derives its name, fluorite typically glows blue but can also illuminate in almost any other color of the rainbow, including white, yellow, red, pink, green, and purple. Working with fluorite is thought to sharpen focus and decision-making skills, as well as increase intuition and open our Third Eye.

7. HERKIMER DIAMOND
Longwave

Herkimer diamond quartzes are not UV reactive on their own, but many contain small amounts of trapped petroleum, which glow a brilliant yellow under longwave. Herkimer diamond's exceptional clarity and formation make it a potent amplifier of spiritual energy.

8. BLUE KYANITE
Longwave, Shortwave

A shy fluorescer, blue kyanite can glow red in UV light. Blue kyanite enhances clear communication, helps us honor ourselves and others, and also serves as a spiritual bridge and meditation tool.

9. SELENITE
Longwave, Shortwave

Some selenites and satin spar varieties fluoresce, like this golden variety from Utah which glows green. Both forms of gypsum are known as clearing crystals, able to energetically cleanse other minerals, the space they are in, and our own energetic fields.

10. SODALITE

Longwave

Traditional blue sodalite may not always fluoresce, but other members of the sodalite stone group do, including the Yooperlites® of Michigan that glow a bright orange, and hackmanite, which fluoresces red-orange.

11. SPODUMENE

Longwave, Shortwave

Spodumene, known as "kunzite" in pink-violet hues and "hiddenite" in green, can actually glow in different shades depending on the wavelength of the UV light. Kunzite signifies love and spiritual awakening, while hiddenite is linked to abundance and growth.

12. WILLEMITE

Longwave, Shortwave

Willemite is known for fluorescing so brilliantly that it was once used in fluorescent pigment production. Glowing bright neon-green, willemite is thought to heighten intuition and spiritual awareness, and serve as a guide in the darkness of our ascension journey.

TOP: Willemite, in daylight, may just look like a common rock. But its brilliant glow sets it apart as a collectible.

BOTTOM: Ruby, fluorite, and mangano calcite are three of the brightest and most commonly recognized fluorescers.

RIGHT: Amber's reaction to UV light is one of the ways to differentiate true amber from resin or copal.

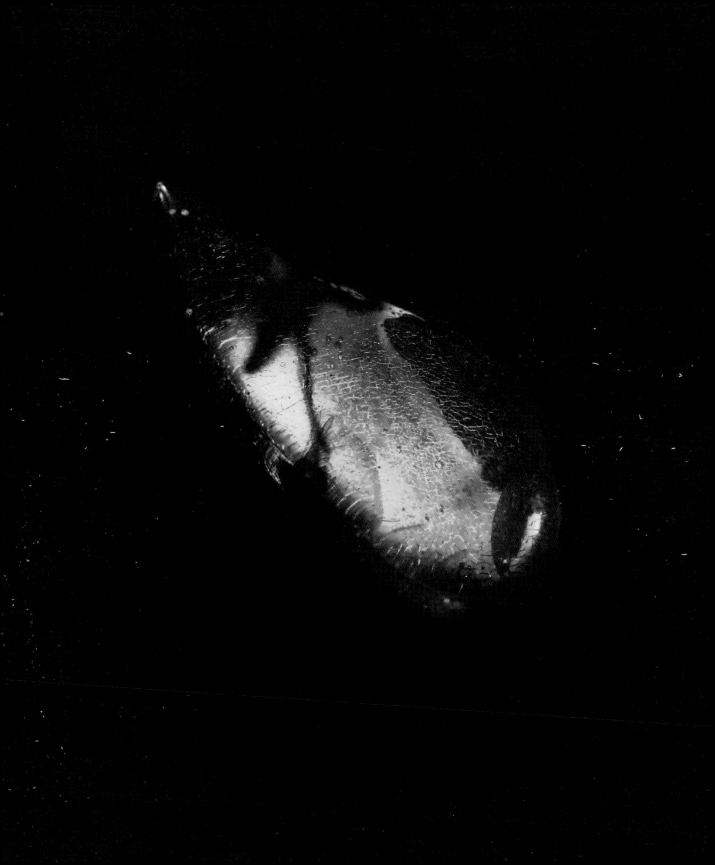

3 BUILDING A LIFELONG RELATIONSHIP
WITH YOUR CRYSTAL COLLECTION

Caring for our crystals is just as important as selecting them with care. While finding that perfect new piece to bring home is always thrilling, a deep satisfaction can be found in integrating these treasures into our spaces, displaying them where they can uplift us every day and we can remember to honor the work we do together.

Noticing when a stone in our care needs to be energetically cleared is a gentle awareness practice to increase our intuition, while seeing to a crystal's needs not only preserves the integrity of its aesthetic and molecular composition, but can also strengthen the bond between stone and keeper.

There's a simple, centering pleasure to be had in dusting, organizing, safekeeping, or beautifully curating our crystals, but we may need some help in knowing which stones require which types of maintenance, especially at the beginning of our crystal-collecting journey. In this section, we'll explore how to clean, clear, store, and display crystals, minerals, and specimens, ensuring a lifelong connection to our crystalline charges.

ESTABLISHING A CONNECTION WITH YOUR NEW CRYSTALS

How you form a relationship with your stones is entirely personal. If you are collecting crystals for purely geological or aesthetic purposes, you might focus solely on what the mineral needs to be displayed safely, or in what ways a stone can enhance the design of a particular room. However, if you have adopted a crystal for its metaphysical benefits, or because you believe in the energy it carries, you may want to honor and establish a connection with your new stone before working with it.

CLEARING YOUR CRYSTAL

Many people prefer to "clear" their crystals when first bringing them home. While crystals are energetically stable beings and do not need to be constantly cleared, you also can't know the exact journey the crystal has taken on its way to you. Therefore, it can be beneficial to help your new stones recalibrate back to their own natural frequency via one of the modalities listed on pages 114–115. If you don't feel your crystal needs this, permit yourself to skip this step.

GREET YOUR CRYSTAL

Once cleared, it's time to introduce yourself to your new gemstone. This can be as simple as saying aloud: "Hello; I'm _____, and I'm really happy to have found you. I hope we can work together on _____." It could also be as complex as an elaborate multi-night ritual. I have included an example meditation here, but there is no right way to greet your crystal, so, as always, check in with what feels right for you.

CONNECT WITH YOUR CRYSTAL

There are many ways to deepen your connection with your stones. Some of my favorite examples include:
- Meditating with the crystal
- Sleeping with the crystal underneath your pillow or next to the bed
- Placing crystals on body layouts and noticing what sensations arise
- Talking to the crystal like a friend
- Asking the crystal questions and being open to an answer
- Looking at the crystal and exploring its physical features
- Using a reflective stone for scrying
- Keeping the crystal with you throughout your day and noticing any changes
- Choosing a name for the crystal

Keep in mind that the more you use, hold, or work with a crystal, the stronger the bond you will have with it, and the more easily its energies can be felt in your life.

INTENTION-SETTING WITH YOUR CRYSTAL

Crystals, energetic beings that they are, never cease exuding their beautiful frequencies. But just like when people come together for a common goal, when we work with our crystals toward a particular purpose, the effects can seem near miraculous. Your crystal found its way to you because you were the one with which it wished to partner. Crystals want to be of use; informing your stone exactly how you hope to heal or expand with its support, or what you wish to change or manifest, will enable you and your stone to align with a common purpose.

To imbue your crystal with your intention, simply hold it in your hands and let it know, out loud, your aspiration. Be sure to phrase this positively (for example, I'm working at my dream job that pays me more than enough to thrive), and if it feels right, sense, imagine, or visualize the crystal lighting up with the energy of your goal, brighter and brighter.

When you are ready, thank the crystal for working with you and place it somewhere that feels appropriate (in this case, the office) or if small enough, carry it with you for whenever you need it. Your stone will naturally hold your specific intention and continue emitting the frequencies of your dreams into the Universe until it is cleared once again.

GUIDED CRYSTAL MEDITATION

This meditation can be utilized to connect with a new crystal, to ascertain how best to work with a stone and its effects upon the mind, heart, or body, as well as to continue building upon an established relationship when support or guidance is needed. Remember, your intuition always knows what is best for you, so adapt and change whatever you need to make it your own.

1. Find a quiet place to sit or lie down with the crystal. Take at least three deep breaths in and out. Before beginning, some people find rubbing their hands together can help awaken the sensory nerve endings. You may become aware of sensations in your hands or body—perhaps a tingle or warmth.

2. Sense or visualize the energy surrounding you—your aura, in whatever color feels most natural to you. The energy circulates out through the top of the head, down to your toes, and up again to your hands, heart, and head.

3. When you can feel the energy within, begin to imagine roots stretching down from your tailbone and your feet, deep deep into the Earth, connecting you to her ley lines and all the minerals buried within her. Imagine that connection—your roots—lighting up and feel her glowing energy traveling up into your body. Notice if any sensations arise.

4. Ask Gaia, your guides, angels, the Universe, elementals, or Higher Self to help you connect with the spirit of your stone. When you feel you have permission, touch your crystal, or if small enough, pick the piece up to keep in your hands, or place on the Heart chakra or the chakra most aligned with your stone.

5. Either in your mind or out loud, greet the stone and offer it gratitude for being with you. Sit with it for some time and allow yourself to open and tune into the frequency of the stone, perhaps visualizing a ray of light the color of the stone reaching out and illuminating your own energy field.

6. Notice any sensations you may feel. Do you feel tingling, itching, warmth, or coldness in your hands or radiating out from the crystal? Are there any twinges of discomfort the crystal is trying to point out? Perhaps all of a sudden you feel energized, or conversely, you feel calmed or even sleepy? Simply notice any shifts without judgment.

7. Next, tune into which, if any, emotions arise. Do you feel joy or happiness? Maybe a buried grief bubbles up, or excitement steals its way through you. Perhaps you simply feel safe. Whatever the emotion you experience, allow yourself to feel it with gratitude.

8. Now you are connected, ask the crystal why it has come into your life, and then listen. Notice thoughts that arise, inspirations that illuminate, sensations, or any wisdom your intuition reveals. Notice if your stone has a "voice," or evokes a specific feeling. Feel free to ask a question, or communicate, either silently or aloud, why you felt drawn to the crystal, or what you hope to manifest or shift in your life with its support.

9. When you feel ready, thank the crystal for finding its way to you, the work you will do, and its wisdom. Offer gratitude to your guides, angels, or Higher Self that enabled the connection, and finally, to Gaia herself for birthing us all, crystals and humans alike.

HOW TO CLEANSE & CLEAR YOUR CRYSTALS

Energetically cleansing and physically cleaning crystals is something that needs to be done every so often in order to maintain the vibrational integrity and potency of your stones, and to keep them looking their best.

Crystals, having much stabler frequencies than ourselves, do not need to be cleansed as often as many believe (so you don't need to haul your crystals out every full moon unless you really wish to). Rather than cleansing, I think of it more as clearing or resetting—the purifying energetic equivalent of shaking it off—and returning the crystal back to neutrality and its unique molecular oscillation rate. Once cleared, the crystal is now vibrating at its most natural frequency and is ready to be worked with again. Opportune times to clear your stones would be:

- Before working with a crystal for the first time to ensure it is free of lingering outside influences
- Between shifting from one intention or purpose to another (that is, "resetting")
- After exposure to very intense energy or emotions, in order to clear the denser frequencies that linger

Physically cleaning crystals can be just as important as, over time, dust, dirt, and humidity can dull the features of stones, especially if they are displayed outside enclosed cabinets.

These are some simple yet effective ways to clear and clean your collection:

ENERGETICALLY

Sound

The easiest cleansing method is using sound vibrations to recalibrate the molecules of a crystal back into alignment. Just as sound can have a profound impact on our nervous system, so too can it be utilized to support crystals. You can use singing bowls (metal or crystal), tingshas, bells, or cymbals, or if you're lacking these ritual tools, even make do with a spoon and a metal pot. Just remember to avoid music made electronically, as the crystals will hold the EMFs rather than be cleared.

Smoke

Humans have been burning sacred plants as a way of ritually cleansing and banishing negative spirits for millennia, and it remains a simple modality for clearing ourselves, our spaces, and our stones. You can choose sacred resins, bark, or leaves directly from your own lineage, work with the plants with which you feel most connected, or even make your own mix or bind your own clearing bundles. Some traditional options include:

- Europe: Rosemary, bay leaves, lavender, and common sage
- East Asia: Cedar, aloeswood, and agarwood
- North/Central America: Cedar, white sage, sweet grass, and copal
- South America: Palo santo
- Africa: Frankincense and myrrh
- India: Guggul or patchouli
- Southeast Asia: Sandalwood and cinnamon

To clear yourself and your stones, simply burn the incense, resin, or dried plants to create smoke, and with intention, either pass the crystal through the smoke several times, or allow the wafting tendrils to surround yourself and the crystals.

Earth

Returning a crystal to the Earth is a beautiful way to allow it to reconnect to the place from which it came. The surrounding earth absorbs any density it may be carrying back into the ley lines of the planet, while helping it reset with its native frequencies. This can be done by burying your crystal in a safe place outdoors, or by filling a clay pot or glass jar with natural soil or sand and placing your crystal within. Keep your crystal there for at least one full day and night, but leave for longer if your intuition says otherwise.

Salt

Salt has been used as a purifying agent for thousands of years across the globe, so it's no surprise that it's a powerful cleansing tool. Clearing crystals with salt works similarly to earthing your stones; simply place dry Himalayan, sea, or another type of natural non-iodized salt in a bowl with your crystals and leave for a full day and night. Make sure to dispose of the salt afterward.

Energy

If you have had training in Reiki or another energetic modality, you can often clear your stones with the same techniques you've learned to clear your own auric field or etheric body. As each methodology differs, be sure to use your intuition while still honoring the tradition from which your energetic practice comes.

Water

Able to physically clean as well as energetically clear your crystals, running water is another simple but powerful option when the hardier pieces of your collection need a quick reset. Crystals with a Mohs hardness of 7 or above can be cleansed in the running waters of a freshwater stream if available nearby, or even your own faucet. Imagine the running water continually carrying away the unaligned attachments the crystal has been holding until it feels renewed.

Crystals

Selenite, satin spar, and halite are all examples of salt-structured crystals that can actually be used to cleanse and clear other minerals. Simply place the stone you wish to clear on (or touching) the cleansing crystal for at least a full day and night. Conveniently, carved towers, bowls, plates, and dishes of satin spar can even be utilized to store your crystals, keeping them continually cleared.

Sunlight and Moonlight

While I prefer to work with the Sun and Moon to aid in "charging" my crystals for a particular purpose, many use sunlight and moonlight as clearing mediums for their stones. Before placing your crystals in direct sun for any length of time, check to see if they are light-sensitive (see page 119), as you don't want them fading. Light-safe stones can be left out in the sun from 30 minutes to all day, while moonlight is much gentler and will never cause your crystals to fade. Simply set them out to absorb the moonlight for the entire night.

PHYSICALLY

Water

Stones with a hardness of 7 or higher on the Mohs scale can be easily cleaned simply by rinsing with water and using a sponge, soft toothbrush, or cloth to gently wipe away the lint or dirt. If your crystal was oiled at some point on its journey to you, the dust might be a little sticky, in which case, add a mild dish soap to the water to ease the cleaning process.

Dusting Cloths and Wands

Crystals on the softer end of the Mohs scale should typically be kept away from water, but wiping your polished crystals down with a microfiber dusting wand will typically do the trick, and can make cleaning your display shelves a breeze as they can fit easily between the stones in your collection.

Compressed Air

Compressed air cans (or for an eco-friendly option, utilize a handheld two-way vacuum/ blower) are particularly useful for the non-polished specimens, minerals, and clusters in your collection. These pieces, while unique and beautiful, can be especially challenging to keep clean, as dust can become trapped in the nooks and crannies where a cloth or duster can't reach. With a press of a button, compressed air gently blows the dust away, preserving the original beauty of the stone.

WATER-SAFE VERSUS WATER-SENSITIVE CRYSTALS

To say a stone is water-safe means that it's both unaffected by getting wet and doesn't harm others if it does. Both are equally important in caring for the crystals themselves, as well as the health of yourself and the environment. Luckily, there are a vast number of water-safe crystals, and these typically share the following characteristics:

- Hardness—A Mohs hardness level of 6-7 or higher
- Non-toxic—Doesn't contain any toxic metals or minerals that can leach into the water.
- Non-metallic—Lacks or only has trace amounts of metals, as higher concentrations of copper, iron, aluminum, and so on can oxidize or corrode with water exposure.
- Non-reactive—Does not chemically react with water.

Even if a crystal falls into all four of these boxes, it's important always to do your due diligence before cleansing a crystal with water, both for the stone's sake as well as yours. These lists feature some of the more popular stones, but are only guides to help you more easily navigate which crystals are water-safe and which are not.

WATER-SAFE CRYSTALS

Durable and easy to clean, many of the most common and popular crystals are actually water-safe. Able to be cleared in running water, utilized in elemental rituals, or simply added to the bath, the following stones are useful for their flexibility and resilience. Please keep in mind that although impervious to fresh water, some of these stones are not safe for making ingestible gem elixirs, and may be sensitive to salt water or extreme temperatures.

Examples

- Agate, various
- Amazonite (briefly)
- Amber (briefly)
- Amethyst
- Aquamarine
- Aventurine, various
- Bloodstone
- Carnelian
- Citrine
- Clear quartz
- Diamond
- Emerald
- Garnet
- Heliodor
- Hiddenite
- Howlite
- Jadeite
- Jasper, various
- Kunzite
- Labradorite (briefly)
- Moonstone (briefly)
- Morganite
- Obsidian, various
- Onyx, black
- Opal (not doublets)
- Rose quartz
- Ruby
- Rutilated quartz
- Sapphire
- Shungite, noble
- Smoky quartz
- Sodalite
- Sodalite (briefly)
- Spinel
- Sunstone (briefly)
- Tiger's eye
- Topaz, various
- Tourmaline, various

ADDITIONAL CONSIDERATIONS

While some crystals are generally considered water-safe or sensitive, individual specimens may have beautiful but random inclusions that affect their interaction with water. It's advisable to research each crystal thoroughly before using it in water-related rituals or practices, such as crystal baths or gem elixirs. When in doubt, it's always safer to use an indirect method: simply place crystals next to water or in a sealed glass container within the water. Both methods inhibit direct contact, which minimizes damage to your crystal and the release of potentially toxic elements. In the end, it's always best to prioritize your health and safety, and that of your crystal collection.

WATER-SENSITIVE CRYSTALS

Stones with a Mohs hardness below 6, evaporites, anhydrites, and crystals that are porous or contain high levels of metals, such as iron, lead, or copper, are typically best kept dry because they can dissolve, crack, become cloudy, or even oxidize as they absorb or interact molecularly with water. While some on this list may tolerate getting wet briefly (e.g. kyanite), many of the stones here can soften quickly (e.g. gypsum), or, although the crystal seems unaffected, can turn the water toxic (e.g. malachite). If you are unsure about a crystal's water sensitivity, use another clearing method.

Examples

- Ammolite
- Angelite
- Apatite, various
- Apophyllite
- Aragonite, various
- Azurite
- Barite
- Calcite, various
- Celestite
- Charoite
- Chrysocolla
- Cinnabar
- Fluorite
- Galena
- Golden healer quartz
- Gypsum
- Halite
- Hanksite
- Hematite
- Hematoid quartz
- Heulandite
- Jet
- Kyanite
- Lapis lazuli
- Larimar
- Lepidolite
- Malachite
- Mica, various
- Natrolite
- Prehnite
- Pyrite
- Rhodochrosite
- Satin spar
- Scolecite
- Selenite
- Talc
- Tangerine quartz
- Turquoise
- Ulexite
- Zeolites, various

LIGHT-SAFE VERSUS LIGHT-SENSITIVE CRYSTALS

UNDERSTANDING LIGHT SENSITIVITY

The Sun is a powerful force in our Universe. It is life-giving, offering us warmth, light, and energy. But the Sun's rays are full-spectrum, and just as solar UV rays can fade paint pigments and damage skin cells, so too can they effect change within our beautiful stones.

Crystals typically grow underground in sheltered darkness, so it makes sense that many cannot be exposed to UV rays without some molecular changes or color fading. While there are mineral types that can withstand prolonged time in direct sunlight, many can begin to fade within a few hours. The sensitivity of a crystal comes down to the stability of the stone, and the presence of specific pigments or trace elements within the mineral's structure. While these lists are by no means complete, hopefully they can be used as an easy reference when deciding where to display and how to clear or charge your crystals.

LIGHT-SAFE CRYSTALS

Light-safe minerals are those that are less prone to fading or discoloration in direct sunlight. Although these color-fast stones are safe to charge or clear in the sun, and can be confidently displayed in well-lit areas without significant risk of alteration, keep in mind that continual, long-term exposure to UV rays can eventually lead to overheating or fading of a crystal.

Examples

- Agates, various
- Amber
- Angelite
- Carnelian
- Chalcedony, various
- Chrysocolla
- Diamonds
- Garnet
- Hematite
- Howlite
- Jade
- Jasper, various
- Labradorite
- Lapis lazuli
- Malachite
- Moonstone
- Obsidian, various
- Onyx, black
- Pyrite
- Sapphire, all colors
- Sunstone
- Tiger's eye
- Tourmaline, black

ADDITIONAL CONSIDERATIONS

Remember, every crystal is unique, and while some might generally be considered sun-safe or sensitive, individual specimens may have distinctive characteristics that affect their interaction with daylight. Rotating their positions periodically can ensure even light exposure.

To preserve the original beauty of light-sensitive minerals, they should be displayed in areas with controlled lighting, or kept in darkened storage when you are not actively working with them. Maintaining the safety and brilliance of a mineral collection requires a bit of care, but it is worth the effort for the joy and support crystals bring to our lives.

LIGHT-SENSITIVE CRYSTALS

Prone to fading, discoloration, dulling, overheating, or cracking in sunlight, these solar-sensitive minerals should be displayed in areas with controlled or indirect light to preserve their original colors. While some crystals may take days to weeks of repeated exposure before the change in their appearance becomes noticeable, others, such as fluorite, can begin to fade almost immediately.

Examples

- Amazonite (fades)
- Amegreen (fades)
- Amethyst (fades)
- Ametrine (fades)
- Anhydrite (fades)
- Apatite (fades)
- Apophyllite (fades and becomes brittle)
- Aquamarine (fades)
- Aragonite, blue, purple, or orange (fades)
- Argentite (darkens)
- Aventurine (fades)
- Barite (blue fades, white turns blue)
- Calcite, various (fades and becomes brittle)
- Celestite (fades and becomes brittle)
- Chrysoprase (fades and becomes brittle)
- Cinnabar (darkens)
- Citrine (fades)
- Clear quartz (cracks with prolonged exposure)
- Corderoite, pink (fades to gray)
- Cuprite (darkens)
- Emerald (fades)
- Fluorapatite/Apatite (fades)
- Fluorite (some localities fade quickly, others fade immediately)
- Gypsum, pink (fades)
- Halite, blue, pink, or yellow (fades)
- Hiddenite (fades)
- Kunzite (fades)
- Lepidolite, purple (fades to gray)
- Morganite (fades)
- Opal (fades, become brittle, and can dull opalescence)
- Phenakite, red (fades to pink)
- Prasiolite (fades)
- Purple creedite (fades)
- Rose quartz (fades)
- Rutile (darkens)
- Scapolite, violet (fades)
- Selenite (dulls)
- Smoky quartz (fades or dulls)
- Sodalite, Hackmanite (red shifts to green, blue, or colorless)
- Spinel (fades)
- Spirit quartz (fades)
- Spodumene (fades)
- Super seven (fades)
- Topaz, various (fades or can change color)
- Tourmaline, various (fades)
- Turquoise (fades)
- Vanadinite (dulls from red to brown)
- Vivianite (darkens)
- Wulfenite (fades)
- Zircon (fades)

WHAT HAPPENS WHEN A CRYSTAL BREAKS?

When a beloved crystal breaks, it can feel like our own heart breaking. While it can bring a sense of loss, it also offers an opportunity for acknowledgment, release, and ultimately healing. When a palm stone splits down the middle, or the tip of a tower chips, the frequency and properties of the crystal itself don't alter. If you were injured, there might be some changes to your emotional state for a time, and the situations around you might need to be navigated differently, but the essence of who you are wouldn't change. The same is true for stones.

There are various beliefs on the meaning behind a stone breaking, including:

- The intention the crystal was imbued with has been fulfilled
- The crystal protected you by "taking the hit" that was coming your way
- The crystal is ready to move on to its next home or be returned to the Earth as it's no longer needed by you
- The crystal wishes to function in a different capacity
- It was just an accident (it happens)

Use your intuition when a breakage occurs to gain insight into the potential lesson that is meant to be learned.

WHAT TO DO WITH A BROKEN CRYSTAL?

Crystals break all the time when growing, with specific formations offering clues to how the crystal repaired itself. Once out of its vug or cavern, the ability to self-heal becomes limited, but that doesn't mean a crystal's journey ends once it's broken. If you feel it's appropriate, you can utilize Loctite, resin, or another mineral-safe adhesive to reattach the fragments. Alternatively, you could repurpose the pieces themselves into something new, or even regift them.

Ways to Repurpose Broken Crystals

- Place water-safe pieces in with your potted plants
- Bury non-toxic crystals in your garden
- Create an aligned intention candle
- Use the smaller pieces to craft or make art
- Wire wrap or electroform to create statement jewelry
- Imbed in resin to make home decor
- Keep the smaller shards to use in grids or layouts
- Gift the crystal back to the Earth as an offering
- Imbue water-safe crystals with an uplifting or healing intention and place near waterways to be carried around the world

Just remember, whether it is repaired, recycled, or gifted back to the Earth with gratitude, the crystal should always be honored.

TOXIC CRYSTALS

Toxic crystals, while often captivating, require careful handling. These minerals may contain elements or compounds that can be harmful, so knowing how to interact with them safely is crucial for both collectors and enthusiasts. Some crystals are perfectly safe to hold, or even to make gem elixirs, but can be dangerous to the lungs if you are exposed to particles in the air while they are being carved or polished. Other crystals are safe to hold, but could be poisonous if ingested. And lastly some stones shouldn't be handled at all, but rather enjoyed from a distance, or kept behind glass. While this is not a comprehensive list, I've included crystals commonly sought out that many don't realize are toxic. Remember, if you come across a new crystal, be sure to research its toxicity level before working with it.

TOXIC IF INGESTED

Crystals on this list are typically safe to hold, keep in a pocket, or wear as jewelry, but can prove toxic and potentially fatal if ingested, inserted or utilized to make gem elixirs. Always use the indirect method (see page 141) for making gem water from these stones, and keep away from children or pets that might swallow them.

Examples

- Amazonite–Copper
- Ammonite–Bacteria, sulfur if pyritized
- Angelite–Lead and sulfur
- Atacamite–Copper
- Aurichalcite–Zinc and copper
- Azurite–Copper
- Boji stones–Sulfur
- Brucite–Asbestos
- Chalcanthite–Copper

- Chalcopyrite–Copper and sulfur
- Chrysocolla–Copper
- Coral–Bacteria
- Covellite–Copper and sulfur
- Cuprite–Copper
- Dioptase–Copper
- Eudialyte (1)–Radioactive
- Gem silica–Copper
- Garnierite–Nickel
- Hematite–Iron
- Lapis lazuli–Pyrite inclusions contain sulfur
- Magnetite–Iron
- Malachite, polished–Copper
- Pietersite–Aluminum, asbestos
- Pyrite–Sulfur
- Serpentine–Asbestos
- Smithsonite–Copper and zinc
- Spinel–Zinc and aluminum
- Sulfur quartz–Sulfur
- Tiger's eye–Asbestos
- Turquoise–Aluminum and copper
- Tremolite–Asbestos

TOXIC TO HOLD

Crystals in this latter category should be treated with the utmost care. If you'd like to wear jewelry made from bumblebee jasper, for instance, be sure the setting keeps the stone from resting against your skin, or check to see if the stone is sealed with resin to reduce the chance of your body absorbing arsenic while it's worn. If you wish to hold galena, wash your hands with soap and water immediately afterward, or better yet, keep cloth or a tissue between the crystal and your skin to minimize contact.

Examples

- Barite–Lead
- Bumblebee jasper (2)–Arsenic and sulfur
- Cinnabar/Cinnabrite (3)–Mercury
- Crocoite–Lead
- Galena (4)–Lead
- Kasolite–Uranium
- Malachite, fibrous–Copper
- Olivenite–Arsenic
- Realgar–Arsenic and sulfur
- Stibnite (5)–Lead and antimony
- Vanadanite (6)–Lead and vanadium
- Wulfenite–Lead and molybdenum

CURATING & ORGANIZING YOUR COLLECTION

As any collection grows, so too does the need for organizing and displaying it. Balancing the desire of easily accessing your crystals can vie sometimes with the dream of creating a beautiful, curated space that showcases the collection as a whole.

Across the following pages are some of my favorite ways to store and display both my personal collection and those for sale in my store, as well as some beautiful inspiration to show you that it's possible to display, organize, and keep your crystals safe—all at the same time.

TIPS, TRICKS & TOOLS TO DISPLAY BEAUTIFULLY

1. SPECIMEN STANDS

Just as there is no end to the variety of sizes and shapes of crystals, so too is there no end to the variety of crystal stands. Three-pronged, four-pronged, swivel, L-shaped, claw, heart stands, LED-illuminated stands: there are a multitude of display options to prop up and beautifully showcase clusters, specimens, slabs, slices, and more, all without damaging the surface of the table or shelf on which they are displayed.

2. FLOATING DISPLAY STANDS

Made of a square plastic frame, these stands open and close securely with a tight but flexible film that holds the specimen in place to make it appear as if it's "floating." Similar to perky boxes, floating stands are perfect for displaying smaller crystals and minerals without the need for an anchoring medium.

3. SPHERE STANDS

A common prop necessary for those round crystals that otherwise would just roll away, sphere stands can be found in a variety of materials such as clear acrylic, stained and lacquered wood, or even metal. From simple rings, to elaborately carved stands, to plush velvet pillows, sphere stands are a beautiful way to display crystalline egg and sphere carvings.

4. "PERKY" BOXES

A favorite of collectors, perky boxes are so called because with the help of putty or glue, the specimen sits upright in the little case. These are standard for small minerals, as the clear plastic box is adept at keeping its contents safe while enabling you to see in from all angles.

5. CANDLEHOLDERS

Another elegant way to display your spheres is by utilizing candleholders. Traditionally composed of metals such as silver, gold, brass, or iron, candlesticks and candelabras are typically made with a round cavity in the capital or sconce meant to secure long tapers, but which is perfect for shapes such as spheres, eggs, or even towers.

6. ACRYLIC/WOODEN MOUNTING BASES

A simple and classic way to display a collection, mounting bases are flat, square, or round stands on which the crystal or mineral specimen sits. Available in a range of sizes, these bases are usually made of acrylic, glass, stone, or wood, with some companies even offering to engrave them so you can always remember the name and locality of your specimen.

7. PRINTER'S TRAYS

A vintage alternative, printer's trays or printer cabinets were once utilized to store the individual metal letters of type sets for printing books, flyers, and newspapers. Either laid flat or mounted on a wall, the small cubbies are perfect for storing, organizing, or showcasing smaller crystals like tumbles, petite specimens, and even towers or carvings.

8. RISERS

If you're curating your collection in a cabinet, I highly recommend a set of risers. Available in different shapes, sizes, and materials, risers allow you to better showcase the variety of pieces in your collection, so none are obscured by another, while also adding flow and drama to your display.

9. MUSEUM PUTTY

A staple for any specimen collector, museum putty—and its cousin, earthquake putty—helps non-self-standing crystals sit upright, anchors minerals to their display base, and can also be placed on sharper edges that may scratch the surface on which a piece is sitting.

10. PLATTERS

For those who want their crystals front and center, or who prefer an artistic aesthetic for their crystal collection, utilizing platters—especially platters made of stone—can be a gorgeous and energetic way to incorporate crystals into your decor.

11. SHELVING

It may seem basic, but literally any flat surface can be used for organizing and displaying a crystal collection. This could be in your bookcase among your favorite books, catching the light on a windowsill (be sure the crystals are light-safe), lending their energy to your desk or in the kitchen, or even more meaningfully, in your sacred space.

A recent trend in the crystal community are handmade wall-mounted display shelves, often beautifully carved into the configuration of mountains, moons, or other sacred shapes that can elevate your stones into a veritable art piece or floating altar.

12. JEWELRY AND TRINKET BOXES

A sweet and lovely way to organize your crystalline jewelry and smaller pieces, jewelry boxes are traditionally cloth-lined with inner niches that are perfect for keeping your stones safe, sound, and feeling special.

13. BOWLS AND DISHES

Decorative bowls are a simple but charming way to keep together your tumbles, spheres, eggs, or palm stones, and, if you so choose, could even be made of stone or crystal itself. Not only do they keep your collection at hand, but your crystal bowl can also serve as a scrying tool—simply ask a question or set an intention, close your eyes, and pluck out a stone to reveal its message for you.

14. DISPLAY AND CURIO CABINETS

Literally designed to display their inner treasures, display and curio cabinets are a classic way to keep your crystals on display where you can enjoy them every day, all while keeping them safely behind glass.

15. UV-LIGHT SHOWCASE

For those who love fluorescent stones, investing in a dark box or cabinet with UV shortwave and UV longwave lighting is a brilliant way to enjoy your stones with natural light—or, with the flick of a switch, watch them glow with an otherworldly luminance.

16. ACRYLIC OR GLASS ORGANIZERS

Available in all shapes and sizes, with cubbies or drawers, on wheels or in travel cases, acrylic and glass organizers allow you to store your small- and medium-sized crystals in the way that makes the most sense for you. I keep mine organized by color, but the possibilities are endless. The inner compartments keep your crystals systematized, while the clear sides or top make it easy to locate the stones you need.

When choosing between acrylic and glass, think about your needs and preferences. Since plastic inhibits the transfer of energy, acrylic organizers are useful for keeping crystals separate that have varied frequencies, while glass has the benefit of being a natural material that can allow the stones to "communicate."

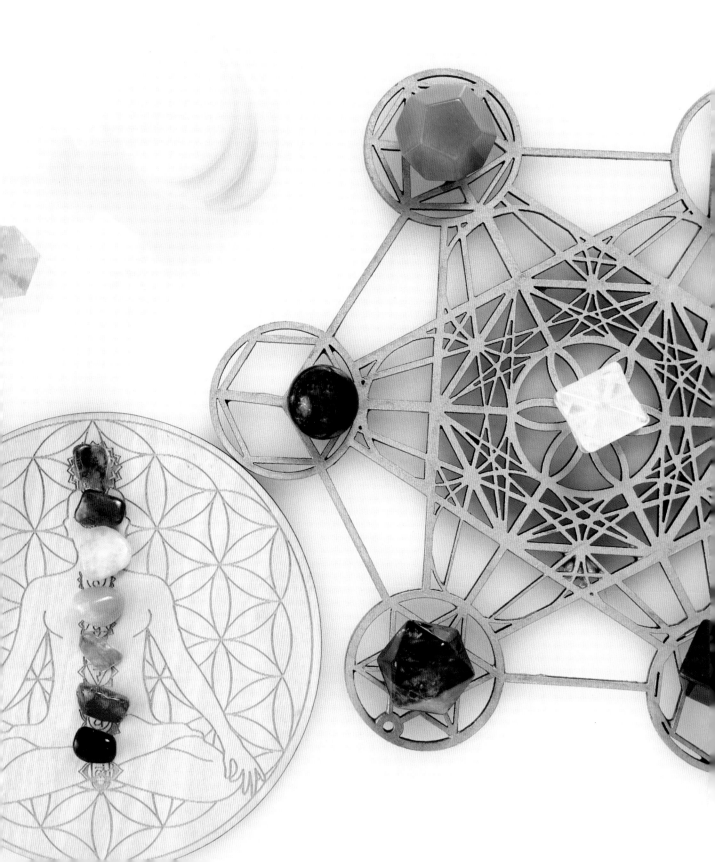

CRYSTAL GRIDS

Sacred geometry is all around us. It can be found in architecture, the leaves and branches of trees, the spiral of galaxies, and in the minute cells of the human body. Many believe geometry provides the container for all of life, and that through the study of sacred geometry we can gain an understanding of the Universe around us, unlocking the very building blocks of creation.

By utilizing aligned crystals in tandem with sacred geometry, we are physicalizing our heart-desires and supporting our own divine ability to manifest. The practice of crystal gridding allows us to communicate our intentions directly to the Universe, in the language of the Universe.

COMPONENTS OF A CRYSTAL GRID

Just as living beings have auras—the energetic torus that surrounds our physical form—so too do crystals. And just as when we gather together in alignment, with one goal, our ability to manifest becomes exponentially more powerful, the same is true for crystals.

Crystals themselves have a perfect crystalline structure: at the microscopic level, crystals are repeating patterns of sacred geometrical formations. Arranging these geometric beings into an intentional geometric grid, empowered by our activation and intention, can create an energy torus much larger, and therefore more powerful, than the sum of its parts.

THE FOCAL STONE

When making a crystal grid, the focal stone—much like our own chakra column—serves as the anchor for the grid's energy torus. Acting as the antennae, the central crystal is what broadcasts your intention into the Universe. The center stone can be clear quartz, or any crystal or mineral energetically aligned with your intention. For example, if you want to fill your life with more love, rose quartz is a perfect center conductor. If you are calling in protection, black tourmaline is a good bet.

The focal stone should generally be the largest piece in the grid or the one with the highest vibrations. For example, you could use a Herkimer diamond, which tends to be small but is extremely high-frequenced. There is no right or wrong shape for the center stone, but being precise can support tapping into your powerful subconscious. If you're starting a new endeavor, for instance, or wish to conceive a child, an egg is a powerful shape to utilize as the focal crystal of your grid.

THE SURROUNDING STONES

These are the crystals arranged in geometric patterns around the focal stone. How many you need will depend on how simple or complex you'd like to make the grid, as well as the basic shape you've chosen. These act as modifiers to the grid and support the specificity of your intention. In a Rose Quartz Love Grid, for instance, you might choose larimar if you want to call in a soulmate, but you'd use rhodochrosite if you wanted to reestablish a more loving, forgiving relationship with yourself. The possibilities are really endless. The surrounding stones also act as satellites, receiving and broadcasting your intention out into the world.

AMPLIFICATION STONES

The amplification stones are often quartz points or tumbles that are placed in a corresponding outer grid, or alternatively placed in geometric points between the surrounding stones. These aren't completely necessary, but quartz serves to transmit, amplify, and maintain the intention of the entire grid.

ACCOUTREMENT

Many people, myself included, often feel inspired to include non-crystal components in their grid. For example, you could use a small item from your childhood, or a photo of a dear one you wish to support. You can incorporate candles, jewelry, or metal or natural elements such as leaves, petals, sticks, or flowers that feel aligned with your intention, or even anoint the sturdier stones with essential oils. In our hypothetical Rose Quartz Love Grid, this could look like incorporating dried rose petals into the geometric pattern we've created, or dabbing a bit of rose essence onto our focal rose quartz. In a Protection Crystal Grid, you could utilize rosemary or basil.

▶ Stability and Protection grid from *Crystal Gridwork* by Kiera Fogg, 2018 (Weiser Books, Redwheel). Elements: Jet, quartz, smoky quartz, red jasper.

HOW TO CREATE YOUR CRYSTAL GRID

CHANNELING VERSUS INTENTIONAL GRIDDING

How to make a crystal grid is one of the questions most commonly asked of me; and I typically begin answering with the caveat: there is no wrong way to make a crystal grid. Although I lay out guidelines here, you know more about your specific circumstances and your intentions than I, and therefore you should always listen to your intuition and the crystals themselves.

This is especially true when channeling a crystal grid. Channeling a grid is simply beginning with a blank slate. Rather than attempting to communicate what you wish to manifest to the Universe, you are allowing the Universe to communicate and manifest through you. This is a beautiful meditation exercise, and can be a powerful practice in learning to surrender, to better hear the stones, and to become more in touch with your inner voice. Channeling a grid can be done with the crystals you have at home or even using items found during a nature walk.

Intentional gridding, as the name suggests, has more steps, as everything is chosen with intention. The act of selection is partly what lends the crystal grid its power, as each decision solidifies what you wish to manifest. I've laid out a guideline here to follow when creating your intentional crystal grid, but I reiterate: these are guidelines, not rules.

1. **Clarify within yourself your intention or what you wish to manifest** This can be something physical (e.g. a new home), emotional (e.g. loving myself more), spiritual (e.g. reconnecting to my Higher Self), or even abstract (e.g. world peace).

2. **Choose the design** Select a design that feels energetically aligned with your intention. For example, if you're calling in more safety, using the stabilizing square geometric pattern will enhance the efficacy of your grid.

3. **Select the stones** Using a reference guide or your intuition, pick out the crystals with metaphysical properties that you feel best encapsulate your desired result.

4. **Choose a location** While some people prefer to align their grid with magnetic north in order to tap into the magnetic ley lines of Gaia, it's not necessary. Simply choose a space that feels sacred or special to you, is unlikely to be disturbed, and is visible to you during your day, such as an altar or a shelf in a bookcase. Avoid electronic surfaces as EMFs can disrupt the energy torus of a crystal grid.

5. **Create the crystal grid** Set up your crystals in the geometric pattern you've previously decided upon (see pages 134-135 for examples). Included here are basic parameters for creating your crystal grid, but remember: there is no right or wrong way. A big part of crystal gridding can be emotion. If you don't feel good about your grid, it won't have the desired effect. Enjoy the process, experiment, play, change it up, and know that by simply building your grid, you're engaging with your crystals, your own intuition, and the Universe itself.

6. **Activate your grid** Activating the crystal grid is an important step for intentional grids that is often missed. This is the moment you, through your divine will, energy, and voice, bring together the separate stones into a unified entity. Some people prefer to use a crystal wand, pendulum, or ritual dagger, but you can just as easily use a metal wand or even your bare hands.

    a) Create a positively phrased statement that summarizes and epitomizes your intention.

    b) Meditate on, journal about, or feel into your desired intention/what you wish to manifest.

    c) Say the statement out loud while directing your wand or hands to the focal stone. Visualize it lighting up with your intention and the influx of energy.

    d) Using your wand or hands, hover over the surrounding stones and amplification crystals in your grid, and visualize a fine web of energy connecting them as you go along, with each stone lighting up as they connect until all the crystals feel unified and energized.

    e) Once the entire grid is activated, visualize/sense the energy torus around it getting larger and larger and larger, moving out into the world. When the time is right, repeat your intentional statement one more time to seal the grid.

    f) Conclude by thanking the crystals for their help in manifesting with you.

7. **Maintain your crystal grid** Crystal grids aren't meant to be a "set it and forget it" tool. You are working in tandem with your stones. Sending the grid a little energy each day, whether that's via a small prayer in the evening, thanking the crystals each morning, or holding your hands over the grid and visualizing giving it a little boost, keeps the grid strong, empowered, and connected to its purpose.

8. **Dismantle the crystal grid** When your goal is accomplished, or you feel ready to release your intention, it's time to dismantle the grid. Don't forget to express gratitude to the stones for their support and thanks to the Universe for co-creating with you.

▶ Samhain crystal grid provided by Linn Krabberød (@SisterSpark_Crystal Grids). Elements: Cornish serpentine, fire quartz, spessartine garnet, black garnet, almandine garnet, carnelian, black tourmaline, black obsidian, black onyx, raw jet, noble shungite, smoky quartz, dravite, oak leaves, Japanese maple leaves, and wheat straws.

CRYSTAL GRID SHAPES

Although the possibilities of crystal gridding may only be limited by our imaginations, sometimes a simple blueprint can help release the fear of imperfection. Let these sacred geometrical shapes guide and inspire; just remember that when your intuition urges, you are always allowed to break the rules and grid "outside the lines."

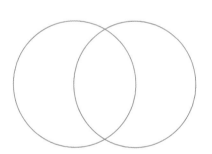

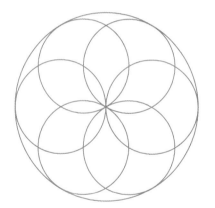

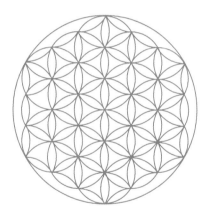

VESICA PISCIS
Choose this grid to...
- Connect to Divine Feminine/Goddess Energy
- Promote rebirth and transformation
- Manifest dreams, ideas, and desires into physical creation
- Engage with Source Consciousness
- Support fertility and engender new life
- Balance and reintegrate dualities (e.g. masculine/feminine, physical body/spirit)

SEED OF LIFE
Choose this grid to...
- Tap into universal creation
- Catalyze new beginnings
- Support new endeavors
- Establish new habits or routines
- Manifest dreams and goals
- Enhance creativity

FLOWER OF LIFE
Choose this grid to...
- Nurture wisdom and inner awareness
- Find harmony, restore balance, and experience peace
- Manifest intentions and dreams
- Tap into the cycle of inspiration and creation
- Stimulate abundance and prosperity
- Connect to the Human Collective/Gaia/Universal Consciousness

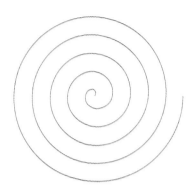

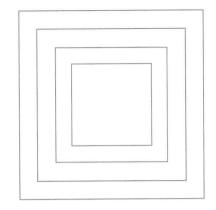

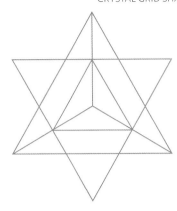

SPIRAL

Choose this grid to...

- Support spiritual expansion and personal growth
- Prompt movement and flow when feeling stuck
- Facilitate finding, selling, or moving homes
- Realign with your purpose
- Stimulate abundance and prosperity
- Grow in a chosen career path

SQUARE

Choose this grid to...

- Increase a sense of safety
- Encourage stability and security
- Build the foundation for goals
- Protect and strengthen the home
- Set and maintain personal boundaries
- Enkindle self-trust and self-confidence

MERKABA

Choose this grid to...

- Activate psychic and spiritual abilities
- Clear and rebalance the chakras
- Accelerate spiritual expansion and ascension
- Facilitate dimensional journeying, astral projection, and shamanic visions
- Enhance spiritual protection and stability
- Balance and harmonize opposing polarities (e.g. male/female, self/divine, Earth/cosmos)

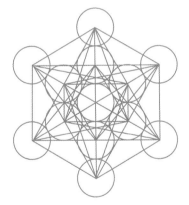

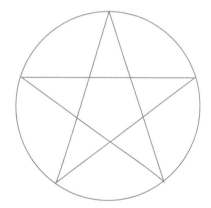

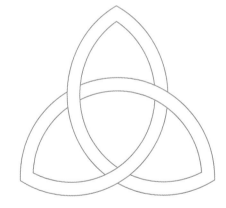

METATRON'S CUBE

Choose this grid to...

- Replace negative thoughts and unaligned habits with loving, expansive ones
- Facilitate growth and inner change
- Access higher levels of consciousness
- Release and heal past woundings and trauma
- Connect to the Akashic Records and remember previous lives
- Communicate with guides, angels, ancestors, and your Higher Self

PENTAGRAM/PENTACLE

Choose this grid to...

- Connect to nature and the five elements: earth, air, fire, water, and ether (Western) or water, fire, earth, wood, and metal (Eastern)
- Reestablish unity and partnership between body and spirit
- Invoke physical and spiritual protection
- Banish negative or unaligned energies or attachments
- Manifest goals and intentions into reality

TRIQUETRA

Choose this grid to...

- Connect to and represent the Triple Goddess (neo-Pagan)
- Connect to and represent the Father, Son, and Holy Ghost (Christian)
- Start a family
- Connect to and represent the three realms of sky, sea, and earth
- Bring a new project or venture to life

CRYSTAL GRID FOR A COMPASSIONATE WORLD

There have been many moments in recent memory where I have watched the news or read online the numerous stories with which we are inundated: war, hate, anger, and pain can feel pervasive in today's society. But I've learned the macrocosm of our collective reflects the microcosm of our individual lives. When we allow ourselves to be subsumed by fear, by anger, by hate, we continue to feed the beast. We can maintain awareness of what is occurring in real time while still focusing on giving our energy to the world we wish to create.

I channeled this grid for a Compassionate World during a particularly low moment of feeling helpless, and I hope in some small way, being published for others to experience, it continues to contribute to a more loving, understanding, and equitable world.

THE FOCAL STONE
- Kwan Yin jadeite carving—Boundless and Enduring Compassion, Gentleness, Serenity, Harmony, Balance

THE SURROUNDING STONES
- **Amazonite palm stones**—Heartfelt Honesty, Compassionate Communication, Self-awareness, Acceptance of Others, Harmony
- **Rose quartz hearts**—Love, Compassion, Connection
- **Lemurian quartz points**—Heart-centered Wisdom, Remembrance of a Loving World
- **Cobaltoan calcite tumbles**—Emotional Harmony, Heart Healing, Uplifting, Trauma Release, Heart-connection, Friendship
- **Emerald (in matrix) tumbles**—Hope, Rebirth, Healing, Compassion for Self and Others
- **Howlite tumbles**—Mind-Heart Balance, Calming of Tempers, Releasing Fear
- **Green tourmaline**—Self-awareness, Self-responsibility, Heart Healing
- **Pink tourmaline** —Emotional Healing, Gentleness, Joy
- **Rainbow moonstone**—Protection, Safety, Guiding Light in the Dark, Intuition, Activation of the Divine Feminine

AMPLIFICATION STONES
- **Clear quartz towers**—Focus and magnify the energy and intention of the grid
- **Clear quartz laser points**—Create cohesion and stabilize the intention of compassion

ACCOUTREMENT
- **Pink rosebuds**—Grace, Gentleness, Joy, Innocence, Gratitude

CRYSTAL GRID FOR AWAKENING DREAMS

When we are fast asleep—our minds quietened—we are most open to our inner world of Spirit. Within dreamtime our guides and ancestors may visit us, roads not taken can be explored, and deep healing can occur. During our nighttime visions, it's not uncommon for inner truths to be revealed as we remember our hidden past, make sense of our present situations, and even glimpse our future.

I created this grid to support spiritual journeying and self-expansion through dreamwork, but moldavite, moonstone, and sugilite are further crystals to incorporate or substitute for the ones shown here.

THE FOCAL STONE
- **Charoite sphere**—Transformation, Spiritual Evolution, Expanded Consciousness, Psychic Abilities, Emotional Healing, Mystical Integration, Dream Journeying

THE SURROUNDING STONES
- **Lazulite palm stones**—Transcendent Awareness, Lucid Dreaming, Revelations, Remembering Dreams, Connection between Conscious and Unconscious
- **Herkimer diamonds**—High-frequenced, Astral Travel, Inner Vision, Connection to Other Dimensions, Higher Self
- **Charoite palm stones**—Transformation, Spiritual Evolution, Expanded Consciousness, Psychic Abilities, Emotional Healing, Mystical Integration, Dream Journeying
- **Vera Cruz amethyst**—Dream Journeying, Lucid Dreaming, Spiritual Protection, Intuition, Ascension
- **Azurite "berries"**—Inner Sight, Psychic Gifts, Past Life Awareness, Connection to Guides, Understanding Dream Symbology

AMPLIFICATION STONES
- **Clear quartz tumbles**—Amplify the energy of Intentional Dreaming

ACCOUTREMENT
- **Jasmine buds**—Spiritual Awakening, Calming, Intuition-enhancing, Meditation, Mindfulness

RESOURCES

WEBSITES

Sage Crystals
www.sagecrystals.com
Store for consciously sourced crystals, minerals, jewelry, and more, plus explore their database of crystal properties

Energy Muse
www.energymuse.com
Store for crystalline jewelry, tools, tumbles, and more, with handy guides to begin your journey

Iris Unique
www.irisunique.com
Learn more about crystal formations and shop for unique pieces

Mind At
www.mindat.org
The world's largest open database of crystals, minerals, meteorites and their localities

Minerals.net
www.minerals.net
Mineral and gemstone guide, community, and gallery

BOOKS

The Book of Stones, by Robert Simmons and Naisha Ahsian with contributions by Hazel Raven, (2021) Destiny Books

The Crystal Bible by Judy Hall, (2009) Godsfield Press

GEM SHOWS

Denver Gem & Mineral Show
September
Denver, Colorado, USA
The second largest gem show in the United States is easy to navigate with 11 different shows across three locations

International Mineral & Gem Show
June
Sainte-Marie-aux-Mines, Alsace, France
One of the world's finest gem, mineral, and specimen shows, drawing over 900 miners and vendors each year

Mineralientage München
October
Munich, Bavaria, Germany
The Munich Show is the largest gem and mineral show in a single venue, with 1,500 vendors across four exhibits

Tokyo International Mineral Fair
December
Tokyo, Japan
Focused on retail versus wholesale, the Tokyo show specializes in rare specimens, high-grade minerals, and collectible crystals

Tucson Gem & Mineral Showcase
January–February
Tucson, Arizona, USA
Largest gem show in the world, with 48 different shows and thousands of international and domestic vendors

GLOSSARY

Akashic Records—a cosmic compendium of all universal events, thoughts, words, emotions and intent ever to have occurred in the past, present, or future in terms of all entities and life forms.

Allochromatic (adj)—having no color in itself, but bearing impurities that contribute color.

Amphibole (noun)—any of a complex group of hydrous silicate minerals, containing chiefly calcium, magnesium, sodium, iron, and aluminum, and including hornblende, tremolite, asbestos, etc., occurring as important constituents of many rocks.

Ascension journey (noun)—the path taken by people who consciously advance toward a greater state of enlightenment or illumination.

Ascension spiral (noun)—the repeating pattern of events that appear in one's life during the ascension journey.

Auric field (noun)—the aura or invisible energy field surrounding living beings as well as inanimate objects.

Birefringence (noun)—see double refraction

Cabochon (noun)—a crystal or gem that is cut with at least one side flat, and polished, rather than faceted, for the use in jewelry.

Chakra system (noun)—the arrangement of the seven chakras within the body; the energetic system from ancient India, in which life force energy moves through spinning "wheels" within the body.

Chatoyant (adj)—having a shimmer or band of reflected light caused by aligned inclusions in the stone.

Chi (noun)—qi; the vital life force or energy that runs through all living beings according to traditional Chinese medicine.

Claires (noun)—psychic abilities, specifically: clairvoyance (sight), clairaudience (hearing), clairsentience (physical feeling), claircognizance (knowing), clairalience (smell), clairgustance (taste), clairempathy (emotional feeling).

Divine Feminine (noun)—Sacred Feminine; the archetypal force and symbol within all living things characterized by its nurturing, receptivity, interconnectedness, expressiveness, and intuition; the balance of Sacred Masculine.

Double refraction (noun)—the separation of a ray of light into two unequally refracted, plane-polarized rays.

Dendrite (noun)—a branching treelike figure produced on or in a mineral by a foreign mineral, typically magnesium.

Evaporite (noun)—any sedimentary rock, as gypsum or rock salt, formed by precipitation from evaporating seawater.

Fibonacci's sequence—a mathematical sequence in which each number is the sum of the two preceding ones; this geometrical formula is known as the Sacred or Golden Spiral and is one of the primary patterns found in nature.

Gem elixir (noun)—a method of energetic infusion in which stones are placed in or near drinking water in order to "program" it with the energetic properties of the crystal in order to facilitate healing.

Gem elixir; direct method (noun)—the process of making gem elixir by placing non-toxic and water-safe crystals directly into drinking water.

Gem elixir; indirect method (noun)—the process of making gem elixir in which a mineral is placed next to or contained within glass that is then placed in water

Hematite (noun)—a reddish-brown to black mineral consisting of ferric oxide.

Higher/Highest Self (noun)—a state of consciousness that can be accessed through meditation and introspection; the omnipotent and eternal part of the soul; the inner guidance that is separate from the personality.

Impactite (noun)—a glassy or crystalline material composed of melted rock and meteoric materials, produced by the impact of a meteorite striking the earth, such as Moldavite.

Kundalini (noun)—the yogic life force that lies like a coiled serpent at the base of the spine; when "awakened" the Kundalini energy can be sent along the spine through prescribed postures and exercises until it reaches the head to trigger enlightenment.

Law of Attraction (noun)—the spiritual belief that the energy one embodies magnetizes like energy to oneself; for example, positive or negative thoughts bring positive or negative experiences into a person's life.

Light code (noun)—energy patterns, imprints, and transmissions that are believed to be encoded into our DNA, crystals, and in sacred locations, or that can be received from spiritual realms as downloads.

Mineraloid (noun)—a naturally occurring, inorganic solid that may look like a crystal, but does not have a crystalline atomic structure, such as glass.

Mohs hardness scale (noun)—a 1-10 scale that characterizes the scratch resistance of different minerals through the ability of a harder material to scratch a softer material, with 1 defined as soft as talc, and 10 defined as hard as diamond.

Nirvana (noun)—in Buddhism, a transcendent state in which there is neither suffering nor desire, and the subject is released from the effects of karma and the cycle of death and rebirth.

Over-soul (noun)—a divine spirit believed to encompass all human souls or sentient beings.

Pegmatite (noun)—a coarsely textured igneous rock composed of multiple types of crystals greater in size than 1 cm. Most pegmatites are composed of quartz, feldspar, and mica, and occasionally tourmalines.

Piezoelectricity (noun)—the ability and process of certain crystals to convert mechanical energy into electrical energy or vice versa.

Polychromatic (adj)—multi-colored.

Prana (noun)—the Sanskrit word for breath, "life force," or vital principle; the universal life-giving force that permeates all beings and objects.

Sacred Masculine/Divine Masculine—the archetypal force and symbol within all living things characterized by action, strength, passion, power, responsibility, leadership; the balance of Divine Feminine.

Sacred Spiral—see Fibonacci's sequence; Golden Spiral.

Schiller effect (noun)—adularescence; the gemological effect of milky sheen, metallic shimmer, or iridescent flash caused by light reflecting off tiny mineral platelets inside the gemstone or from the diffused reflections of light from parallel intergrowths of the stone.

Schumann frequency (noun)—7.83 Hz; the dominant frequency of the Schumann Resonances, a range of electromagnetic waves that exist in the Earth's ionosphere, formed by the interactions between the planet's surface and the ionosphere, that are created through lightning strikes, which act as a trigger for the resonance to occur.

Tektite (noun)—any of several kinds of small glassy bodies, in various forms, produced by the impact of meteorites on the Earth's surface. See impactite.

Universal Consciousness (noun)—a metaphysical concept suggesting an underlying essence of all being and becoming in the Universe.

Universal Source (noun)—that from which all energy and life derives; God, Spirit.

Vagus nerve (noun)—longest and most complex of the cranial nerves that runs from the brain through the face and thorax to the abdomen and controls digestion, heart rate, breathing, and the immune system.

Vedic Astrology (noun)—the sidereal astrology tradition derived from the ancient Vedic and Hindu texts of India.

Zeolite (noun)—any of various hydrous silicates that occur as secondary minerals in cavities of lavas, and can act as ion-exchangers; any lab-grown hydrous silicates that are identical to naturally occurring zeolites.

INDEX

ACKNOWLEDGMENTS

When one speaks of writing a book, it is often compared to birthing a child. There is so much heart, soul, patience, and time for it to gestate, and so much labor required to bring forth the new creation. Support is viscerally needed when a parent is giving birth: loved ones to care and encourage, midwives, elders, or doctors to ease the process or step in to help if necessary. So too, is assistance and encouragement vital to the author, especially one publishing her first book.

So, I'd like to take this moment to thank those who either directly contributed to the creation of The Crystal Collector, or without whom I'd never have completed it.

Firstly, the entire team at Quarto, in particular Kate Kirby, who initially reached out to collaborate on the eve of her retirement; Charlene Fernandes, my ever-patient editor, who continued to encourage me and graciously fought to extend deadlines when my world fell apart; and Martina Calvio, who made this book into a thing of beauty. Secondly, I'm so grateful to my publisher, David and Charles, for believing in me and The Crystal Collector, and for wanting to bring it to the world.

On a more personal note, I want to express my appreciation to my parents, who always encouraged me to be curious, to question, and to always look for my own answers. I'm especially grateful for my mother, Jacqueline, who was a phone call away whenever I needed to cry, because, let's be honest, I cried a lot.

I am forever indebted to the entire Sage Crystals team, and to Miranda most of all, for keeping our crystalline company going as I spent half a year focused on bringing The Crystal Collector to life while also going through divorce proceedings.

I have to also acknowledge my circle of incredible friends who kept my spirits buoyed while also keeping me accountable; this is especially true of Tara and Melissa, both of whom endured an inordinate amount of texts as I counted down each and every page I finished; Harumi, Mariana, and Danielle, who let me vent and kept me sane, as well as Coda, my writing buddy who almost single handedly got me through the final chapters.

I'd also like to thank: my mentors, Marla Mervis-Hartmann, Wendy Luttrell, and Holly Herbig, who each have helped me live in a more aligned way; my core of strong-willed aunties and godmothers; and my heart: Missy, my beloved pup without whom I'd honestly be lost.

Lastly, I want to acknowledge the beautiful Sage Community: Thank you, each of you. There is no way this book could have been birthed without you.

CREDITS

Sage Crystals (crystals used in the book: www.sagecrystals.com); The Fossil Cartel (supplemental crystals used in the book); The Crystal Spirits (image 3, top left, page 125: www.crystalspirits.co.za / @thecrystalspiritssa); Tiffany Willardo (image 3, middle right, page 125: @designsbytiffanyw); Jennie Brinegar (image 5, page 125: www.allthatshimmerzz.com / @allthatshimmerzz); MadMagicShop (image 11, page 125, 127: madmagicshop.com / @madmagicshop); Blissful Moon Co. (image 1, 14, page 126: blissfulmoon.co.uk / @blissful.moon.co); Jel of @jellyycharms (image 10, 13, page 125). seaseasyd/Shutterstock.com; Cavan-Images / Shutterstock.com; vetre/Shutterstock.com; ju_see/Shutterstock.com; eloresnorwood/Shutterstock.com; Minakryn Ruslan/Shutterstock.com; Linn Krabberød (image 133: @SisterSpark_CrystalGrids); E.Va/Shuttertock.com; vvoe/Shuttertock.com.